What others have said about the **first edition**,

A Primer for Beginning Teachers in Secondary Schools:

The best organized and interesting staff development book I ever read. Your knowledge and enthusiasm about the new teacher is contagious.

Tom Dicks
Assistant Principal, Supervision & Administration

The primer seems to be a practical launching pad for beginning teachers, one that is consistent with theory.

Associate Professor Susan Weybright
Department of Education
Goshen College

A very good book for secondary students.

Professor Fannye E. Love
Chairperson, Department of Education
LeMoyne-Owen College

I want this reference book only an arm's length away from my desk. This is must reading for every teacher new and master as well...It can save years of trial and error experimentation in the classroom.

Margaret Denora
Mathematics Teacher

This primer is a useful tool in helping individual's beginning their teaching careers in secondary education.

Defense Activity for non-Traditional Educational Support
DANTES: Book Review, August, 1994

TEACHING
and the Art of
SUCCESSFUL CLASSROOM MANAGEMENT

S E C O N D   E D I T I O N

A HOW-TO-GUIDEBOOK FOR TEACHERS IN SECONDARY SCHOOLS

HARVEY KRAUT

 AYSA Publishing, Inc.
Staten Island, New York

TEACHING AND THE ART OF SUCCESSFUL CLASSROOM MANAGEMENT

A How-to-Guidebook for Teachers in Secondary Schools

By Harvey Kraut

Published by: *Aysa Publishing, Inc.*
P.O. Box 131556
Staten Island, New York 10313 U.S.A.
Phone & Fax: (718) 370-3201

First Printing 1994
Second Printing, revised 1996

Printed in the United States of America
Library of Congress Catalog Card Number: 96-83576
Kraut, Harvey
Teaching And The Art Of Successful Classroom Management: A How-to-Guidebook for Teachers in Secondary Schools/by Harvey Kraut
Includes Index
ISBN 0-9640602-2-1: $16.95 Softcover   Canada $21.95

Table of Contents

Brief Version

A teacher prepares students to meet their responsibilities in a democratic society.

Table Of Contents

About the Author

Mr. Kraut has been a classroom teacher for thirty-three years. His entire career has been in the secondary public schools of New York City. He is a licensed Assistant Principal Supervision and Administration, and has taught at the university level.

This book is the outcome of the author's decision to share his expertise with others, particularly those about to embark upon a secondary school teaching career as well as those newly arrived in the profession. *Teaching and the Art of Successful Classroom Management* is a "how-to-book" for teachers the contents of which set a foundation for successful classroom instruction.

Mr. Kraut earned his B.A. degree from Indiana University, Bloomington, and both the Masters in History and Professional Certificate in Administration and Supervision from Brooklyn College.

Acknowledgment

Appreciation is extended to my wife, Joanne, and children Lisa and Daniel for taking much time from their busy schedules to assist in reviewing the manuscript.

I am fortunate to have had my preliminary draft *Teaching and the Art of Successful Classroom Management* reviewed by many caring people who have assisted me greatly with their suggestions and expertise. A special thanks to the following education professionals: *Dr. George J. Petersen, Bowling Green State University; Assistant Professor Susan Weybright, Goshen College; Dr. Lorene Painter, Lenoir-Rhyne College; Associate Professor Roger A. Stewart, Boise State University; Dr. Geoffrey Coward and the Department of Education staff, Wagner College.* Their sensitive comments and encouragement are appreciated in the preparation of this second edition.

The daily responsibilities and duties of a teacher are numerous and fragmented. While the veteran teacher is able to "shift gears" to easily accommodate the range of required activities, a first year teacher is more likely to become overwhelmed and to feel extremely frustrated.

Teaching and the Art of Successful Classroom Management (2nd. ed.), presents to the new secondary teacher a fundamental outline of the many tasks and responsibilities that they will encounter during their first year of teaching. While the book does not go into depth, it does successfully incorporate anecdotal and practical examples that guide the reader through these essential teaching activities. The topics in this book are appropriate and necessary, especially for beginning teachers and are presented in a clear and straight-forward manner. Very user-friendly!

It is obvious that the author, through numerous years of experience and observation, fully understands the needs of teachers. He has taken the complex daily routines of teaching and presented them in a practical and easily adaptable format for first year teachers as well as anyone else who may be thinking about becoming a teacher. I recommend this book to any student who is currently in an education program or who will be entering into their first year of teaching.

George J. Petersen, Assistant Professor
Department of Educational Administration and Supervision
Bowling Green State University

WARNING DISCLAIMER

This book was created to provide instruction for teachers in secondary schools. It is offered solely with the accepted acknowledgment of the buyer that the author and publisher render information only to complement other educational sources. The teacher is best served by further inquiry into the sources of classroom instruction in secondary schools from other available educational sources.

Effort has been taken in the preparation of this book to make it clear and concise. There may, however, be errors in both content and printing. The book, therefore, should be viewed as a tool and not an absolute source of information for classroom instruction.

The author and Aysa Publishing shall not be liable nor responsible to any individual or institution for misusing the contents of this book.

If you do not wish to be bound by the statement above, please return this book to Aysa Publishing for a refund.

Introduction

This book is written in behalf of all secondary school teachers. It serves as an instructional guide for novice teachers and teachers-to-be. It is also a vehicle for evaluation and change for those who are already experienced professionals of the classroom.

The content material reflects thirty-three years of personal experience in teaching and supervision. During your careers you will discover teaching methods and techniques not discussed in this manual but which work to your satisfaction. This text, therefore, is not to be viewed as dogma but only as a launching pad toward classroom competency.

If you are a teacher-to-be or one newly arrived to the classroom, you undoubtedly have acquired much educational theory from university study but possess relatively little in the way of practical classroom experience. If you have participated in a student teaching program you have, in addition, acquired some experience necessary for instruction but still lack many needed skills for teaching competency. A teacher is someone who conveys information to others, but it is a master teacher who has the ability to institute methods and techniques for making others into active receivers of information. Further, he/she is capable in getting these receivers to internalize information for both present and future uses as well.

The book is designed to assist all teachers in making others receptive to information. A specific aim, however, is to give the new or inexperienced teacher a "jump start" in the classroom by offering him/her a foundation upon which to build classroom experience.

The content begins with the school term's "opening day" and proceeds, step by step, with instructions for conducting basic classroom activities and teaching. At its conclusion, there are exercises involving typical classroom problems for analysis and useful teacher forms. It is hoped that this text serves you well in your careers. Good luck!

Another school year begins!

Chapter One

ESTABLISHING CLASSROOM OPERATIONS

Do not fear opening day! The youngsters you are about to meet are as excited and apprehensive as you are. The majority eagerly await their new classes and are determined to have a fresh start with both a new subject and teacher. Each student aspires to succeed in spite of any previous disappointment or failure!

Preparation. To be prepared for the initial meeting the teacher might consider using transparencies and an overhead projector for discussing classroom rules and course objectives. One who is unfamiliar with this teaching tool can find assistance from a supervisor or buddy-teacher sometime before opening day. In addition, sets for one's classes of course-outlines, class rules, grading policy, and homework procedures should be prepared for distribution. Included with these class-sets are signature request forms for parents and guardians to sign acknowledging their review of student materials. These forms are to be returned to the teacher the next day. The instructor safely maintains them for the term. This procedure establishes an important link between the classroom-teacher and the student's family the very first day of school. The preparation time is worth the instructor's efforts, for it can alleviate student-teacher misunderstandings should they occur during the term. In addition, the following items are needed for the first subject class meeting:

1. a blank seating chart [see Teacher Form B]
2. chalk and a chalkboard eraser
3. an introductory lesson plan which explains your classroom rules and grading system [full explanation to follow]
4. copies of the department's, or your own, homework assignment sheets which are to be distributed if time permits [see Chapter Four]. If your initial introduction takes the majority of the period, hold over the homework sheet distribution for the next day. Your Assistant Principal may have informed you that textbooks will be distributed at an appropriate date and time. If such is the case, postpone homework sheet distribution until the day before textbooks are dispersed.

Supplies. The following supplies should be on hand for immediate need and should be housed in the teacher's classroom desk:

a. a box of chalk
b. an extra board eraser
c. rubber bands of different sizes
d. a writing pad
e. note paper (3" x 5")
f. paper clips
g. a stapler and staples

h. extra pencils and pens (several red and green)
i. a ruler
j. scotch tape
k. thumb tacks

The room closet should store the following materials for future class needs:

a. a ream of 8 1/2" x 11" white lined paper
b. " "   " "   "   unlined paper
c. a variety of colored unlined paper to be used for decorative backgrounds on bulletin boards
d. several sheets of white oak tag
e. short 5" x 7" paper to be used for short quizzes
f. a class set of pencils
g. a set of blank Scantron forms if your school has a Scantron marking machine
h. overhead projector transparencies and appropriate writing pens

It is not imperative that all of the above be in your closet on opening day. Eventually, have these resources available so that you need not become frantic when some items are unexpectedly needed.

Seating arrangement. As your students enter the room, allow them to sit where they wish. Take attendance from your class list or whichever class information sheet has been made available to you. Call student names and record their presence or absence. Once attendance is completed, ask if anyone has difficulty hearing your voice or seeing the board [you wrote your name upon the chalkboard before class began]. Assign youngsters with possible hearing or vision problems to seats in front of the room. Make a notation to check the health records of such students, at a later time, to determine whether or not a hearing or vision problem is indicated for them. Should none exist notify both the health office and the home of your classroom findings and request a follow-up. Discourage friends from sitting next to each other. Inform students that you reserve the right to alter seats anytime during the term. Distribute the blank seating chart [see Teacher Forms] after first explaining where you wish students to print their names, in the appropriate boxes, along with their home telephone numbers. This is an important first step in associating both a student's "face and name" for the seating chart becomes a teacher reference for student identification at the second day meeting. After having met all your classes you will be ready to enter student names and telephone numbers into an official class grading book. This is done during your leisure time. However, you might want to wait a day or two until additional new admits or discharges have become finalized.

Classroom procedures. Your activities, for the past ten minutes of your introduction, have not gone unnoticed. The youngsters before you have already discovered that the teacher is highly organized. An opportunity now exists to demonstrate a no-nonsense approach to your classroom learning process. Using an overhead projector, chalkboard, or reading from the distributed classroom sheets discuss, with the youngsters, the ground rules for classroom procedures as follows:

1. Your classes are always conducted in mutual respect. When the teacher is teaching everyone is listening. If a student is speaking everyone is, once again, listening.

2. There is no calling out. When one wishes to speak one raises a hand.

3. Each student is to purchase a loose-leaf binder (8 1/2 x 11 inches) along with two blue or black pens. These are to be brought to class daily. Inform the class that you do not provide "handouts"

or pen replacements for those without their own writing tools. A student without a pen at the start of a lesson sits for the period. Remind them that it is always best to have two pens in case one runs out of ink.

4. Daily homework assignments are noted at the right of the front chalkboard. Each homework has an assignment number which corresponds to the assignment on the homework sheets. Remind the class that each assignment is due the following day for collection. Distributed homework sheet assignments should be neatly cut with a scissor and the appropriate assignment scotch-taped to a sheet of loose-leaf paper beneath one's name. Answers to questions are written in full sentences beneath the printed as-signment. The student need not recopy homework questions [see model in Chapter Four].

5. A student is permitted to miss no more than three home-works per term. After three homeworks are missed, there is a penalty for each additional one not completed. When a student is absent he/she is to continue with the additional homeworks; one for each day's absence. If a student is too ill to do homework a note from a parent must be presented explaining the cause of the absence. All missed homeworks are to be made-up [the teacher will decide how best to collect absentee homework for grading].

6. The class can anticipate homework four to five times per week.

7. All classroom rubbish is to be discarded at the end of the period. As you exit the room throw away undesired items into the trash basket. No one is permitted to discard waste materials after the period begins.

8. Eating and drinking is not permitted in class.

At this point stop and ask if there are any questions. There may be a need to clarify still further. Usually students request an additional review of homework rules. Be sure you fully understand the criteria you have set down for your students. Once the clarification period is completed, you are ready to explain the grading policy.

Grading policy. The grading policy is based upon a point system. It reflects the total performance of the student and alleviates the often difficult task of objectively determining a student's final grade at the end of the term. Grading a youngster based primarily on the teacher's perception of student performance is no longer totally necessary. The final grade is not finalized by the teacher's so-called "toss of the coin." Student feed-back in the past has demonstrated that youngsters respect the grading system as a valid indicator of their overall achievement in the class.

Direct the class to staple or scotch tape, at home, the distributed grading policy sheet into their notebooks. Next, write the following scheme upon the chalkboard:

4 full period tests	= 4 x 100 =	400 points
8 short quizzes	= 8 x 10 =	80 points
1 midterm	= 1 x 200 =	200 points
1 report	= 1 x 100 =	100 points

Total Class Value		780 points

In addition, inform your students that for each homework missed, after the three permitted, 5 points will be deducted from the total at the end of the term. Also, for each misconduct mark noted by the teacher, from his/her record book, there will be a deduction of 5 points from student totals.

After the youngsters have copied the scheme, ask for questions. Some, if not most, will appreciate a fuller oral explanation of the grading system that you have presented. Explain as follows: "As of this moment I cannot be sure of the number of exams to be given, with any certainty, during the term. However, let us assume that the figures on the chalkboard will be the final number for the term. About a month before the term ends, I will read all student grades to you including the excesses in missing homework and demerits. You will then summate all the points you have accumulated during the term. I will then go to the chalkboard and place a scheme like the one you have just copied, but which accurately reflects the term's work, upon the board."

At this point anticipate some student asking, "But how do I know what final grade I've earned for the class?" Your explanation is as follows:

$$\begin{aligned}
\text{Total Class Value} \;=\;& 780 \text{ points} \\
65 \text{ is the minimum pass} \;=\;& \text{x.65} \\
\hline
& 507 \text{ points}
\end{aligned}$$

Five hundred seven points are necessary for the minimum passing grade. To determine the number of points representative of a 70, 75, or an 80, one multiplies the total class value by the decimal value of .70, .75, or .80.

Point system clarification. To clarify a bit further, offer the class a scenario of a fictitious student's grade performance:

John Jones' Performance in Physics I
Tests: 73, 82, 63, 87
Quizzes: 8,5,7,10,4,9,9,6
Midterm: 76 (multiplied twice because of the
             importance of the exam)

23

Report: 80
Missing homework in excess of the three
permitted: 2
Demerits: 2
John's total performance= 595 points minus 20 (for
missing homework and/or demerits)= 575 total
points for the term.

Had the total class value been 780 points, John would have earned between a 70 and a 75 grade. In such a situation both the teacher and the student will reach agreement, for finalizing the grade, during the end of term conference [see Chapter Ten].

Once again, ask the class if there are any questions. Inform students that they are to return the cut-off with parental or guardian signatures the next day. Tell them that a copy of the distributed rules sheets will be posted upon the classroom bulletin board as a reference. Next, spend a few additional minutes querying the class, once again, for questions which may still need clarification. Call upon several youngsters to reiterate important points to remember regarding each of the areas discussed during this first class meeting. After this has been completed, and there is adequate time, you may want to begin distribution of the Uniform Homework Sheets [see Chapter Four]. So ends your opening day. You're off to a great start!

Chapter Two

CLASSROOM MANAGEMENT AND
PREPARING TO TEACH

The majority of novice teachers enter their first classroom encounter armed with methodology from various sources. This often creates for the teacher a state-of-mind best described, as one of confusion. In some cases inept or uncaring supervisors place a new teacher into a lion's den believing that he/she will learn the art of instruction along the way. The new teacher is given token information, the basic necessities for getting his/her classes under way, and then cast into an arena comparable to an ordeal under fire. The following unit on classroom management is absolutely vital for initial teaching success. The information permits the new or inexperienced teacher to enter a classroom with both confidence and direction. The chapter's methodology is basic to that of any secondary school environment in the nation.

Classroom priorities. Each teacher sets an order of priorities for his/her classroom. The teacher who spends the first six minutes talking to one or more entering classroom students, while twenty-five or more youngsters are gathered about discussing the previous night's sports results, and/or a boyfriend/girlfriend dilemma, is going to confront an unruly beginning class period. This teacher has not considered his/her classroom priorities carefully. A daily routine of priorities, therefore, should be observed to avoid any disciplinary problems.

Beginning of classroom period. Assume the previous period has just ended. Both you and your class are coming together from other rooms. Upon entering the room, place your belongings on the desk, take your daily lesson plan to the chalkboard, and write "Aim:" with its lesson number above it. Teachers with a penmanship problem or who find it difficult writing upon the chalkboard, should consider using an overhead projector when convenient. This classroom tool offers a teacher the additional advantage of not having to turn one's back to the class, thereby averting possible discipline problems. Next, place the day's homework, or nightly assignment, at the far right front chalkboard as noted by the following model:

> Homework
> Class: French 2
> Do: Assignment #16
> Due: Thur., 3/7/96
> Reminder- Quiz next Tues. covering
> in-class lessons 12-16 & homeworks 11-16

Return to the first board with the inscription "Aim." Be sure you have informed the class that "all notebooks are open and everyone is copying from the front boards." At this point you have not yet written the lesson's Aim on the chalkboard. There is a reason for this. The lesson's Aim is to be elicited from the class at some point during the instructional period and is then placed upon the board. This is done to assure the youngsters' attention and to keep them focused upon the lesson's development. However, experience has shown that this pedagogic operation can be somewhat difficult depending upon the academic mix of the classroom population. If students are academically poor in basic communication skills, the teacher can still succeed in eliciting the lesson's Aim from the class by using content questions that clearly relate to student needs. In such a class, eliciting the Aim directly from youngsters is vital toward uplifting instruction; it challenges weaker academic students to perform at a level of higher thought.

Motivation. Beneath the Aim of your lesson is a motivational device. The motivation may consist of almost any "vehicle" which puts students into a frame-of-mind for the lesson. It may be a quote, a set of instructions to do something, a stick figure cartoon, a series of pictures or photographs along the chalkboard ledge or a stimulating review question that bridges past lessons with the one for the day.

Beneath the "Aim" identify the motivation for your class. To do so you might use the terms "Warm-up" or "Do Now." Place your motivational question, instructions or other device here. Your front boards now have an "Aim," a "Warm-up" and the day's homework assignment. As the class copies the front boards you are now ready for the next step.

You are now free to take the daily attendance without disruption [be sure to observe attendance-taking procedures for your school district]. Once attendance-taking has been completed address yourself to school-wide announcements if there are any. Be sure to speak briefly toward both motivating the homework assignment for the day and in reminding the class of any upcoming tests, quizzes, reports or other matters you deem important.

Homework collection. A special word about homework collection. A teacher cannot in all honesty collect homework from each of five classes [this is usually the case for teachers in large American urban secondary schools] and painstakingly grade student papers four or five times per week. It is too grueling a task and a teacher would have little time for his/her family or personal recreation. Rather, make your students aware that you have adopted a system in which homework is collected from scattered rows on any given day. Inform students that they can be certain homework so collected will be carefully examined and graded by you. Explain the collection procedure to the class as follows:

"After attendance is taken I will ask who did not do last night's homework? Students who attempted the homework but did not complete it, because of some difficulty with it, will not be penalized. They must show me proof of their efforts. If you did not do it, you must inform me of this before I announce those rows from which homework will be collected. This includes students who have been absent unless they have brought a parental excuse note. If I am not notified of missing homework, and I call your row for collection, you will be marked for both the missing homework and for failing to inform me of it."

The aforementioned student-confessional is valuable in that it serves to strengthen the teacher's desire to teach trustworthiness as a social value. By having established honesty as a value in the classroom, the majority of students will hereafter oblige you with a show of hands when homework is not done. There will be a few, however, who early in the term will test both you and your procedure. You will discover as the term progresses that when a youngster is caught without homework, he/she is often "ridiculed" by the class. Do not accept an excuse from a student for not having done homework. Mark him/her accordingly in your record book. Once the entire class knows that you "mean business," by being consistent in your classroom management, students will act more responsibly. The above steps should be "digested" thoroughly by the teacher. They provide for classroom order! Once you have "routinized" your steps, youngsters will come to view you as an efficient leader of "their classroom." The so-called "teaching battle" is half won at this point.

Room appearance. Your room should also reflect your content area. A "Current Events" bulletin board should be displayed at a convenient location in the room to which you have been assigned for the majority of your teaching assignments. Similarly, the room should reflect student papers that demonstrate good test scores, writing samples, drawings, and other academic accomplishments. At a minimum, demonstrate a positive sample of each student's performance once during the term. Make the room pleasing to the eye and comfortable to be in. Students will come to think of this classroom as their "second home." Social studies and language arts instructors could use news-magazine covers, book-jackets and/or posters from travel agencies for their classrooms. One method of securing interesting display materials is by communicating with foreign embassies. Many embassies are pleased to forward materials for classroom use. Teachers of science, mathematics, foreign languages and other subjects could secure materials from organizations in their respective academic or vocational areas. A bulletin board or displays section should also be created for the posting of school and/or guidance announcements.

A teacher demonstrates respect for young people.

Chapter Three

MAINTAINING THE CLASS RECORD BOOK

Maintaining a concise and accurate record of student performance so that the teacher and others clearly understand its contents, often eludes the good intentions of many inexperienced secondary school instructors. In many localities, the class record book is a legal document reflecting both classroom attendance as well as student performance.

The subject teacher should be cognizant that all personal markings and encodings in the record book should be easily identified by all school officials, inquiring parents and officers of the courts should questions arise about a particular youngster. Often, class records contain a wide gamut of dots and dashes, positive and negative symbols, letters of the alphabet [upper and lower case], vertical and horizontal arrows and an assortment of geometric figures. As a rule of thumb, teachers should make all markings clear and simple. They should record only that which is relevant in determining the student's total class performance. Illustration # 1 is a hypothetical model of how the teacher might organize his/her class record book. The book's preparation can be undertaken before meeting one's classes for the term. If a teacher has multiple classes, be sure to calculate an adequate number of blank record book pages, for each class, for maintaining the entire term's attendance.

Abridged Model of a Class Record Book

PERIOD 3 NAME	OFF MEMO	QUIZ 1/2	QUIZ 3/4	QUIZ 5/6	QUIZ 7/8	TEST #1	TEST #2	TEST #3	TEST #4	MIDTERM	PROJECT	FINAL EXAM	REPORT CARD 1/2	FINAL GRADE	OCTOBER 5	6	7	8	9	12	13	14	15	16
ADAMS, MIKE	8/3	6/9	7/8	10/10	7/7	85	79	84	76	80	93	P	89/80	85	•									
AMORE, NICK	8/3	Eyes														H								
ANDREWS, SARAH	8/3																		#H H					
ATWELL, JOHN	8/3	Asthma																	a					
BLACKSTONE, DAVID	8/3																	a.						

Illustration #1

The names of students in each of the classes can be entered several days after a term begins or when school programming has been completed. Until then, the teacher may take attendance on sheets of paper headed with the subject title, the recitation period, and the date. Each day a new attendance sheet is passed around the subject class room. Beneath the heading students print their names and affix their written initials alongside. The instructor must take care not to lose or misplace these sheets for attendance figures from them will be entered officially into the record book.

Illustration #1 is composed of several suggested codes [shorthand means of entering notations quickly] which makes it relatively simple to indicate student information and performance. At the extreme left are the names of students in a fictitious period 3 class. To the right of the names are the official class and homeroom designations. These designations are necessary when entering report card grades and/or in locating a student when he/she is not in the subject class. This section is followed by a narrow "Memo" column that may be used as a reference for noting any special health, vision or hearing problems of youngsters.

When preparing your record book assume, for example, that the teacher will offer 8 quizzes and 4 full-period tests during the term. To save space, quizzes are separated from each other by a diagonal line. See Illustration #1 once again. The illustration shows all grade entries for a term. Following student name, "Mike Adams" along the horizontal, it is noted that he received a grade of 6 [of 10 possible points] for quiz #1 and a 9 for quiz #2. The columns labeled "Tests" signifiy exams having a possible value of 100 points. These are full period in-class or take-home exams. This section is followed by columns headed "Midterm," "Project" [book report, oral presentation, research paper or other special assignment] and by a space for entering a final or comprehensive exam score [pass or fail].

In many secondary schools, youngsters are given three report cards each term. Each term's final or third report card grade is the one usually recorded on a student's permanent record [note the report card section of the record book]. For example, John's final report card grade was an 85.

The extreme right section of Illustration #1 demonstrates daily class management entries. The section is headed **OCTOBER** and represents the fictitious numbered days, the "5th through 9th." In the center of columns dated "6, 7, and 8," one notes the entry "#10, #11 and #12." These are the homeworks collected on the 6, 7, and 8th of October. The *dark dot or bullet* [inscribed in blue or black pen] under October 5 indicates that student "Mike Adams" received a demerit for discipline or some particular behavioral incident and that "Nick Amore" did not have his homework when the subject teacher collected assignment #11. Homework is indicated by an *upper case H* written in red pen. Further, "Sarah Andrews" failed to inform the teacher of her not doing homework, when #12 was collected, and was given a *double H* as a penalty. The record book, in addition, demonstrates that "John Atwell" was absent on October 9 [absences entered as a lower case "a" in red pen] and that "David Blackstone" was at first marked absent for October 6, but came to class late.

To show a late notation, the teacher places a blue or black ink diagonal line through the red lower case "a" and writes a lower case "l" [for late] above it in blue or black ink. If a student has been absent and brings an excuse note for the absence/s, the instructor merely circles the absence "a" in blue or black pen. The circled "a" indicates the absence was explained by either a note from the home or from an attending physician. If a student has missed the subject class because of a school-related function but has given the subject teacher an officially approved note explaining the absence, the teacher places a blue/black pen line through the absent "a" and writes EX [excused] above it.

These are all the codes one needs! The teacher should staple or tape a "key" of the codes to the inside cover of the record book where it may be easily found by others. The aforementioned recording system permits a teacher to answer a variety of questions concerning a youngster's performance in his/her subject class. The instructor should maintain class records for at least one year after a term's end. This is a safeguard against grades being lost or entered incorrectly upon a student's permanent record.

Teachers are important role models for youngsters.

Chapter Four

THE DAILY LESSON

The daily lesson plan is a necessary tool for teaching a successful lesson. A well prepared lesson plan, with all its necessary components, is like having a master-teacher with you in class. In many school localities a teacher is required to submit his/her weekly lesson plans for a supervisor's inspection. Ideally, this inspection serves the function of having the supervisor note both the lesson's weaknesses and strengths and then make recommendations which would assist the teacher in achieving satisfactory performance. In recent years, teacher unions have contractually won new rights for teachers that permit them the freedom of bypassing supervisory personnel for the weekly observation of such plans. Whichever is the case in your geographic area of employment, the lesson plan still remains a critical component in the quest for excellence in teaching!

Developmental lesson. A variety of lesson types may be used daily by secondary school teachers. One type used frequently is referred to as the "developmental lesson." This lesson consists of approximately nine components. These components are:

    a. the lesson's objectives
    b. materials needed
    c. the Aim of the lesson
    d. the motivational device
    e. the homework assignment
    f. preliminary questions
    g. a medial summary
    h. pivotal questions
    i. a final summary

An examination of each of the above terms would provide us with an understanding of their role in the classroom lesson.

Lesson objectives. Typically, every lesson has lesson objectives. What exactly then is meant by a "lesson's objectives?" Objectives may be defined as the lesson's goals. They can be demonstrated by student performance and can be evaluated by the teacher upon completion of instruction. A teacher strives to achieve specific academic goals during his/her lesson. For example, during a mathematics lesson, the objectives or goals might be:

1. the class will be able to define the meaning of "numerator" and "denominator."
2. the class will be able to add simple fractions with similar denominators.
3. the class will be able to add simple fractions with unlike denominators.

Similarly in a social studies class, where an aim might be related to the early Industrial Revolution, the lesson's objectives or goals could be:

1. the class will be able to give three causes of the Industrial Revolution in England.
2. students will be able to name three early inventions in the British textile industry.
3. students will be able to explain why British farmers moved to cities.

Lesson materials. "Materials" pertains to those items which are needed to assist in achieving a lesson's objectives. In a science class one might need a Bunsen burner, several flasks, test tubes and litmus paper. In a history class you would want an appropriate map of the nation under study for a particular period, source materials if called for and perhaps composition paper for a specific in-class writing assignment. Such necessary materials are noted in one's lesson plan. They serve as a reminder of things needed on hand with which to conduct the lesson.

The lesson Aim. An "Aim" of a lesson is a statement informing the class of a lesson's purpose. It is always written upon the chalkboard as a question to be answered. For example, in an English class studying William Shakespeare's Othello, an appropriate Aim might be, "How shall we interpret the personality of Iago?" It is important that the teacher state the Aim in terms which assist in personalizing it for the class. Thus, personal pronouns such as "you" and "we" are generally, when possible, incorporated into the Aim question. Additional examples of Aims for different lessons [for a variety of academic subjects] might be:

"How do we solve fractions involving binomials?"
"How might we become wiser consumers in the market-place?"

"What were the outstanding and immediate problems confronting both the British Parliament and the American colonists in 1775?"
"How do we solve pulley problems in physics?"
"What are the chemical properties of salts?"
"How did Mark Twain use symbolism in Huck Finn?"
"How do we conjugate irregular verbs in French?"
"What are the physiological components of the human cell?"

Before eliciting an Aim from a class, the teacher must first introduce his/her lesson by the use of preliminary questions. Generally, preliminary questioning is the vehicle which begins class discussion. Once the teacher has guided class discussion to the point where an Aim can be derived for the day's lesson from one or more students, he/she then asks the class, "Can someone state the single most important question to be answered in today's lesson?" At times it may become necessary for an instructor to assist the class in stating an Aim more clearly than first offered by a variety of student responses. The teacher need not, however, spend more than a minute or two in eliciting the daily lesson Aim.

Motivational device.   The purpose of the motivational device has previously been discussed in Chapter Two. Whichever device is used, it must succeed in getting students into a frame-of-mind for the lesson. To achieve this goal, the motivation must stimulate immediate interest for the class. Several examples of motivations that stimulate high interest are discussed below.

A singular device that offers particular success in launching a lesson is to create a cartoon using stick figures. For example, in a European History class the teacher might draw a cartoon [if the lesson was concerned with the Russian Revolution of 1917] as noted in Illustration #2. Such a cartoon acts as an "attention-getter," for student eyes become fixed as the teacher places it upon the chalkboard.

Such a stick figure drawing serves several educational purposes. First, it calls upon students to do a cartoon analysis much in the same manner that a newspaper reader might reflect upon an editorial caricature. Secondly, it bridges what was previously taught with the material to be learned in the forthcoming lesson. Thirdly, it draws attention to particular events, by the use of stick figure comments, accompanied with other labeled clues.

Other techniques are available for incorporation into a variety of lessons. A mathematics teacher might use the following motivation upon the chalkboard:

Do you remember how to solve problems involving multiplication of binomials? See if you can do the following, using your class notes if necessary:

$$(3x + 2d) (2x - 4d)$$

Illustration # 2

A science teacher could offer the following instructional "Do Now" or "Warm-up" to a lesson's introduction:

I have placed a test tube, a beaker, and a flask at your lab stations. Before beginning today's lab experiment, weigh each of the distributed items using the metric scale on the laboratory table top and record each of the respective weights (in grams) into your notebooks.

These are merely three examples of suitable motivations teachers may use in specialized academic disciplines. It is left to both the teacher's imagination and creativity to deal with other additional types as demanded by his/her respective daily lesson plans.

Homework. Homework, too, plays a vital role in the daily lesson. In Chapter One, a proposal was made for the use of pre-written term homework assignments. Although some teachers might consider preparing their homework assignments on either a weekly or even daily basis, pre-written term homework assignments have advantages that outweigh preconceived disadvantages. Their strength lies in making students aware of term responsibilities and in permitting them to plan ahead in order to satisfy the requirements of the term's agenda. In addition, it provides absentee youngsters with a continuing link to the classroom. However, a novice teacher undoubtedly needs additional time before undertaking the writing of a full term's homework. Such an instructor could prepare uniform homework sheets covering only one or two weeks of subject content. In such a scenario, a beginning teacher would provide his/her classes with homework sheets listing only 4-8 assignments at the first meeting of the term. Additional assignments could then be distributed at a later date either on a weekly, or bi-monthly, basis.

Uniform homework assignments are not the absolute they appear to be. The classroom teacher has the flexibility of modifying or delaying these assignments at any given time. All that is necessary is that the teacher inform the class that a "uniform homework assignment is being delayed and a new one is to be done instead of # 23 [an example] of the uniform homework sheets." Once again the instructor places the new assignment on the chalkboard in the appropriate location and assigns it a number, being sure, in addition, to motivate its completion.

It is vitally important that a teacher understand the educational importance of homework assignments. Being a teacher, you are interested in improving both student study habits and skills. Providing good homework assignments assists young people in developing positive study habits and prepares them for independence in learning. Homework permits growth in written expression and is effective in having students learn the methodology for using both research materials and techniques. The classroom teacher has the important responsibility of both determining and providing instruction for basic study techniques that students need to succeed, both within the classroom and the world at large.

Uniform homework preparation. If your academic department does not make use of uniform homework, and it is the school's policy that each teacher prepare his/her own assignments, then you should seriously consider its incorporation within your classroom. Prior to the beginning of the term, and once you have secured your new class assignment, secure a copy of the class text. Based upon the mandated curriculum to be covered by the subject teacher, preview the text and determine which areas you wish to cover for the term. Pre-read those chapters for which you will be assigning homework. As you read a chapter, jot down questions which your students eventually will be answering for homework. Label each assignment, with its set of questions, with a homework number. As you write your questions, keep in mind that homework is not mere busy work for youngsters. You are interested in developing skills that students need. Your homework should help them to read for information, to analyze a problem, to use charts and graphs, to evaluate cause and effect relationships, to learn to outline content material and to build an adequate vocabulary. For a school term of twenty weeks duration, you should plan thirty to forty homework assignments. This figure takes into consideration school holidays, vacation periods and special school days.

The set of homework sheets, which you distribute at the beginning of the term, should also provide students with a directional opening paragraph of instructions. It might appear as follows:

GLOBAL STUDIES 4: UNIFORM HOMEWORK SHEETS

Students are to use the aims, pivotal questions and homework assignments for each lesson. These questions contain specific knowledge, understandings and skills needed to master the lesson. Students are required to answer questions in their homework subject section. They are also expected to demonstrate mastery of these questions during the classroom lesson. If a student is absent, he/she is expected to continue with the assignments until his/her return to the subject class. Replacements of lost homework sheets will not be provided by the teacher. Copies will have to be made from classmates. Keep your sheets in a safe place at home for your use. All readings and assignments have been keyed to the text World History, Smith and Jones, Stone Book Company, Inc., 1996.

Beneath the directions, list your homework assignments. Note that each assignment has a homework number, pages to be read, an Aim and pivotal questions to be answered. Be sure you do not overload students with an assignment. Each night's homework should take a student no more than forty minutes to one hour to complete. An assignment might typically appear as follows:

#1 How did the Congress of Vienna change the map of
Europe?
(read pp. 306-10)

1. Why was the Congress of Vienna established in 1814-15?
2. Who were the more important nations represented at the Congress? Who were their spokesmen?
3. What were the rules of "compensation" and "legitimacy" established at the Congress?
4. What was Czar Alexander's proposal for a "Holy Alliance?" Would you have supported it had you been a representative to the Congress? Why or why not?
5. In your opinion, how did the Congress destroy both the ideas of democracy and nationalism?

The aforementioned homework model involves a directed reading approach. The assigned text pages have been teacher previewed. The result is a series of questions that guide students through much factual information but which narrows in upon specifics vital to subject development and understanding. The teacher, of course, is not limited solely to this type of an assignment. The homework could have questions requiring interpretation of textual material that culminate in the writing of essays. In addition, there could be assignments that involve the preparation of maps and/or statistical information and data. Such decisions are left to the discretion of the individual classroom teacher.

Grading homework. The teacher must be cognizant of the need to both adequately review and grade student homework. Teacher feedback must be on-going! It is a vital vehicle for student motivation and for helping youngsters to succeed in the classroom. Numerical grades need not be assigned to corrected homework. Rather, a code-mark such as a check, check-plus or check-minus at the top of the completed front page of homework may be used to indicate the teacher's evaluation of a student's effort.

Of particular importance is the instructor's comments upon the written homework page. Comments should not be written in red, for students perceive red inscriptions as rigidly authoritative. Instead, a green pen could be substituted for this purpose. At a minimum, the teacher should write one positive comment upon the last page of a student's homework. This writer has observed that positive notations, more than suggested criticism, result in heightened student motivation and both improved classroom participation and test scores. When the instructor writes a positive comment he/she acknowledges the student by his/her first name as follows: "Nice job, Mark!" "Terrific progress, Mary!" and/or "Super homework, Joe!"

The information in this chapter is preliminary to the actual task of teaching the lesson. The teaching portion is commonly referred to as a lesson's "development." It is to this topic that we next turn our attention.

The teacher prepares students for responsible citizenship.

A teacher prepares students with skills vital to the workplace.

Chapter Five

DEVELOPING THE LESSON

Reviewing. The day's lesson generally begins with a brief review of material previously covered both in class and/or including the night's homework. The teacher led review attempts to facilitate an orderly transition into the new lesson's content. This transition is smooth and unimposed by the instructor. It is not rushed! When successful, the review bridges previously learned information with the day's new topic. The teacher begins the review by asking the class "could someone summarize the important conclusions [reference to previous class notes is permitted if necessary] made in yesterday's lesson?" This question is student-centered and usually invites active participation. In addition, the review assists previously absent students in determining the current status of course content being discussed in class. After classroom participants have given a brief but adequate summary [this may take 3-4 minutes], attention then turns to covering the day's new content. The teacher's task is now to move from the simple to the complex. In a "developmental lesson" this is accomplished with a series of key questions. The questions should be linked to both the lesson's Aim and its motivation. Remember that questions are clear, simple in tone, and generally personalized by the pronouns "you" and "we." They are also adapted to student interest, experience and need.

Questioning technique. The novice teacher is advised that questioning technique will not be mastered in a day, week or month. Good questioning technique develops with continuous class-room exposure. To get a "jump start" in mastering this technique, there are rules to be followed; several specific "do's and don'ts." These are noted as follows:

Question Types To Be Avoided

1. Do not ask a question in which the response can be a mere "yes" or "no" or a single word answer. Example: "Do you agree that Napoleon's invasion of Russia was a mistake?"
2. Avoid double or multiple questions. Example: "Was Edgar Allan Poe a good storyteller? Which do you feel is his best tale and why do you think so?"
3. Avoid vague questions. Example: "If I place sodium chloride into the solution, what happens?"
4. Do not ask "tugging" questions. Example: "Well, he was correct in taking the action which he did, wouldn't you agree?"
5. Avoid "teacher talk" after a question. Example: "What chemical reaction is produced when you add sulfuric acid to a metal? Oh, you remember a gas, and what else did we learn?"

Good questioning technique is clear, to the point, and personalized. Questions are addressed to the entire class. They invoke thought! They may also be introduced by the words "how" or "why." The teacher should allow a lapse of several seconds (5-8), after asking a thought provoking question. This permits youngsters to "internalize" the question, before answering.

Examples of good questions, in several academic disciplines, are:

1. "Look at yesterday's class notes. In your opinion, explain which you consider to be the more important cause of the Seven Years War."
2. "Why do you think mathematicians use letters such as X and Y when they refer to numerical values?"
3. "Describe what you see when the litmus paper touches the solution of sodium hydroxide."
4. "Why do you think it would not be a wise investment to purchase municipal tax-free bonds during a period of inflation?"
5. "Had you been a member of the French Third Estate, how might you have responded to Louis XVI attempt to seek foreign intervention during the French Revolution?"

The goals of good questioning are many. Basic to all instruction is the desire that students learn the material content being taught. There are, however, other pedagogical reasons as well.

Classroom socialization. The teacher should stimulate socialization within the classroom by striving for creative thought and having students communicate clearly with one another. Student participation, in and of itself, is never adequate. There is a need for "quality participation" which creates a classroom aura of enthusiasm, interest, and sharing. An atmosphere of classroom democracy and "citizen" rapport, is a goal to be achieved! Good questioning technique becomes invaluable in attaining this goal. The teacher assists the development of "quality participation" in several ways. His/her personal qualities of appearance, clarity of speech, animation, humor, poise, and knowledge of subject matter all add to the classroom climate of well-being. The instructor also strives to "reach" each student in class during the class period. This is best done by creating a series of questions which lead to a "teacher-to-student" to "student-to-student" answer response.

Good teaching is crucial to student success!

There is generally a need for the instructor to enhance classroom socialization by stimulating the learning environment. This is accomplished by appropriately redirecting student responses to questions. The teacher achieves this by calling upon students to offer input to a previous classmate's response. Patience is required of the teacher when confronted by students who fear to speak in class. If there are no raised student hands to call upon, the teacher stimulates debate by simply asking, for example, "Mary, why do you agree, or not agree, with Mark's statement?" or "Anthony, what can you add to what Mark has already told us?" The instructor strives to avoid a "teacher-to-student" to "teacher-to-student" response environment. If you discover routinely that such is the case, recheck questioning technique. The problem more than likely lies here.

Preliminary and pivotal questioning. The series of preliminary and pivotal questions represent the core of a lesson. The teacher's preliminary questions are those that attempt to elicit basic lesson information from the students. They are generally straightforward in their handling of the content material. After three or four such questions, the instructor evaluates what has been discussed in class by using the chalkboard to write a "medial summary." This is often done by simply asking students to "summarize what has been learned in today's lesson." Under a topic heading write your student responses, being careful, however, to correct poor or poorly worded answers. The instructor should also acknowledge student contributions to the summary effort.

Your pivotal questions are more complex in that they strive for a deeper critical evaluation of the material under discussion. Pivotal questioning provides the more sustained exchange of classroom ideas. Make use of the chalkboard to record student responses to these questions. The chalkboard notes are recorded under one or more topic headings. They can be recorded in outline form or some other organized manner acceptable to student needs. Chalkboard notes are always legible and are written in satisfactory prose. It is also preferable, when writing an outline, to use short sentences rather than single-word notations.

Classroom time. The teacher must be aware of classroom time. A lesson is divided into teacher-determined time frames so that it is completed within a prescribed class period. For this to occur, the teacher must be cognizant of the time devoted to each of his/her classroom functions. This is not an easy task but can be achieved with continued classroom experience. Without meaning to appear contradictory, however, the experienced teacher knows that lessons are occasionally carried over to a following class meeting. The instructor always confronts the dilemma of a lesson going beyond the given class period. There are probable causes for this to happen. An unusual number of lesson interruptions by non-classroom monitors carrying school-related messages, unexpected classroom emergencies, unannounced fire and shelter drills and stimulating classroom discussion are only a few reasons lessons may have to be extended.

The latter reason is one over which the teacher has control. At times, a decision has to be made whether to terminate a lesson in the desired time frame or to allow discussion to continue. Given this choice, it is preferable that a learning situation, marked by "heated" debate, be allowed to continue to the classroom bell. A "final summary" can be used as the motivational device in the next lesson with a new lesson being introduced, shortly thereafter, by a *submotivation*.

Chapter Six

LESSON TYPES

Lesson formats. Nothing detracts students more than having their teacher use the same lesson format repeatedly. Variety is the spice of life, and within the classroom this rule applies, too. You need not confine yourself to a daily "routinized" lesson style. At one's disposal are a variety of lessons of which the developmental lesson is only one. What follows is a diversity of lesson types, but by no means all, offered to familiarize and inform the instructor of his/her classroom options. Each of the following has a lesson number, an Aim and a motivation just as with all other lessons.

Open book. The open-book lesson requests that students do a particular task using a text or other textual source along with teacher-directed instructions. Such a lesson can be individualized or broken up into mini-groups of two or three students. Talking among youngsters is permitted provided they stick to the task at hand. The teacher becomes a resource person who walks about the room and assists students with questions or other lesson-related problems. A time frame is provided for the completion of the assignment, which is then followed by a question-and-answer session and a final summary outlined upon the chalkboard.

Role playing. The role playing lesson involves young-sters' portraying historical, contemporary, or fictional personalities related to some specific event and involving a particular academic discipline. In a history class studying the causes of the French Revolution, the teacher might assign one group of youngsters to pre-pare a script in which they role play French peasants airing their grievances against King Louis XVI. Later, these same students would, on an appropriate day determined by the teacher, make their presentation to the class. Role playing becomes an extended motiva-tion for the lesson. It may also be initiated as an introduction that acts as a bridge between what has been previously learned and the content material about to be studied.

In a science class, the teacher might, for example, have a stu-dent present Galileo's discoveries concerning gravity and the planets before a group representing the Catholic clergy. Upon culmination of the role playing, the teacher has the youngsters write their observa-tions upon paper, has a reading of several papers and then allows time for discussion and summary.

Classroom debate. The debate lesson stimulates a higher-order of classroom thought. The teacher is encouraged to use this lesson type to more deeply explore classroom topics with his/her subject students. The teacher initiates this lesson by undertaking a question or issue to be debated by classroom teams. He/she selects volunteers, or assigns class members into teams. Students often shun debating before members of the class. The instructor should reassure his/her students that there is nothing to fear by speaking in public.

Overcoming students real or perceived fears requires considerable tact on the part of the instructor.

A teacher, undertaking a classroom debate for the first time, might have student team members selected by a hat-draw. Generally, selected teams are assigned a debate-position to a question or issue. Teams usually consist of 3-6 members, each of who is responsible for preparing a specific aspect of a question or issue that supports the team position. A selected team leader both directs and coordinates the team agenda for the upcoming debate. The teacher informs the selected teams of the date for the debate.

The teacher decides whether he/she is to be the debate moderator or to have a student act as one. The instructor prepares debate rules and teams are informed of this information. A time frame is established for this classroom experience, too.

The student audience is responsible for listening and taking notes. At the termination of debate, class members may ask questions of team members or the teacher may decide to begin review and summary proceedings. Debate information is student-summarized. The instructor structures class responses under appropriate headings upon the chalkboard. This lesson can be followed-up, during an additional period, with an in-class writing exercise or short quiz. These choices are left to the discretion of the classroom teacher.

Cooperative learning. The cooperative learning lesson is a new variation of the group learning scenario. The cooperative learning experience is a valuable one for both students and teacher. Through a concerted effort to work together as a class, although class members are divided into small groups, students gain the advantage of the socialization process by learning both content material and problem-solving techniques. They become eager to have their group compete against others in the class. As a result, youngsters that participate infrequently are enthusiastically encouraged, by their team members, to become more active participants. It is the teacher's role to coordinate, direct, and shape such activities. The teaching goals of a cooperative learning lesson are as follows:

1. To have students socialize as a team of "players."
2. To have each team member recognize his/her responsibility to the team effort.
3. To have the team solve a specific problem.
4. To encourage the team to offer and weigh a variety of options in problem solving.
5. To have the team demonstrate either through written or verbal communication, its findings and conclusion.
6. To coordinate and present the findings of all teams.

The teacher interested in learning extensively about cooperative learning is referred to several sources.[*]

How to begin a co-op lesson. A cooperative learning lesson begins by dividing students into groups of four or five. This may be done randomly at an initial outing. Once the teacher establishes the academic mix of his/her classroom students, future lessons are planned with greater participant balance. Committees should be

---

[*]Johnson, D.W., & Johnson, R. (1975). *Learning Together and Alone: Cooperation, Competition, and Individualization.* Englewood Cliffs, NJ: Prentice Hall.

Johnson, D. W., & Johnson, R. (1983). "The Socialization and Achievement Crisis: Are Cooperative Learning Experiences the Solution?" In L. Bickman (Ed.), <u>Applied Social Psychology Annual 4</u>. Beverly Hills, CA: Sage Publications.

Cooperative Learning Center, David W. Johnson and Roger Johnson, 202 Pattee Hall, University of Minnesota, Minneapolis, MN.

composed of academically strong and weak youngsters sitting together as a group. After several cooperative lessons during a school term, the teacher might permit students to vote on whether they wish to remain with the same committees intact or reorganize for future co-op lessons.

Each committee selects a team leader and a secretary. The team leader is responsible for assuring the completion of the team's assignment. He/she is also responsible for assuring the participation of all committee members in discussion and in the evaluation of the task at hand. The secretary's role is to record the committee's findings. The secretary reads final committee findings to the members, who may offer revisions. After all revisions have been completed, each team member records the secretary's final version into his/her notes. The teacher reserves the right to call upon any team member, in response to his/her inquiry concerning the assignment, to explain both team answers and/or opinions when the task is completed. The team grade is an average score based upon each team member's participatory contribution whether it be verbal or written. A teacher may also evaluate a committee's performance by questioning individual committee members or offer a short quiz to the entire class that tests what has been learned. The instructor should be mindful that individual student accountability is an important educational ingredient of cooperative learning lessons.

Models for cooperative learning. The following are two model lessons, which can be used in World History and Economics classes, using cooperative learning techniques. Each model is offered in hopes of familiarizing the teacher with the style of the cooperative lesson.

MODEL I

Lesson # 11

Aim: What was the impact of Renaissance thought upon Western man?

Objectives:

1. Students will be able to describe two ideas of the humanist, Pico della Mirandola, 1463-94.
2. Students will be able to write one descriptive paragraph telling about da Vinci's views on art.
3. Students will be able to describe two ideas of Desiderius Erasmus for Church reform.
4. Students will attempt to predict two future outcomes resulting from Renaissance thought.

Materials: Prepare student copies [for distribution] of the following reading selection excerpts:

> *Oration on the Dignity of Man*-Mirandola
> *On Painting Versus Poetry*-da Vinci
> *The Praise of Folly*-Erasmus

Motivation:

Discuss the following: What do you think?
"Renaissance thought altered the course of European history!"

Procedure: Break class into co-op committees. Distribute three prepared copies of the reading selections [one of each] to a team. Have the committees discuss the selections and the questions asked. Have each committee submit a fact-finding sheet [answers to questions] along with the names of all committee members. Inform committee members they are to copy committee answers, when finalized, into their notebooks. Announce the date of a short essay quiz [a teacher option] concerning the co-op assignment.

<u>Questions</u>

1. *In the opinion of the committee, how does della Mirandola demonstrate his reverence for man?*
2. *In your opinion, why does da Vinci claim that painting is a higher form of art than poetry?*
3. *List 3 ways in which Erasmus criticizes the Church.*
4. *Based upon the 3 selections you have read, what socio-political predictions would you make for the future of Western Europe?*

The model for the second co-op learning lesson is used over a longer time frame than the typical single or double period group setting. It is established as a longer-range group project of from one to two periods per week and is ongoing over two to three weeks in duration.

MODEL II

Lesson # 23

Aim: How do we establish a small business venture?
Objectives:
1. Students will learn to be innovative in formulating a small business venture.
2. Students will learn that many people are involved in establishing a small business.
3. Students will learn the meaning of marketing, the sources for securing capital, and the role of management in operating a small business.

Materials: Prepare student copies of the sheet below.
Motivation: The distributed sheet is the motivation.
Procedure: The class is divided into teams and the following sheet is distributed after the Aim has been placed upon the chalkboard:

Committee Project

The class will be divided into teams. Teams will meet twice a week for about two weeks. Dates will be announced by the teacher.

This project is worth 100 points proportionally divided between team members. Each member will contribute points toward the team grade. Thus, a team of five members will each contribute up to 20 points of the total for the final project grade for his/her team. A non-performing member can lower a committee grade thus resulting in team failure. Remember, this project is a team effort just as in the real business world.

Any team with a legitimate complaint against an uncooperative member may make a formal request to me [the teacher] in writing, signed by three of the five team members, requesting a member's removal. If after consulting with the accused I find grounds for his/her removal, the team member will be removed and given a zero grade for an exam equivalent.

WHAT IS TO BE DONE?

- Each team will select a chief-executive officer [CEO] to coordinate all discussions and who will be responsible for conducting team affairs. A chosen team secretary shall be responsible for submitting the final team project to the teacher for a grade at an appropriately announced time. The team secretary shall be rewarded with an additional 5 bonus points if he /she acts responsibly.

- Each team member shall be assigned one of the individual projects listed below. He/she will be responsible for submitting his/her project neatly written to the team CEO after all committee decisions have been discussed and finalized. This will be done on 8 1/2" by 11" paper [loose-leaf is permitted]. The individual's name and project title will appear at the top of the page.

- The committee secretary shall coordinate team papers and then prepare a brief description of the business venture. The secretary will also read the final copies, to be submitted to the teacher, one additional time to committee members prior to their copying the reports into their notebooks. The two or three paragraph description of the business venture written by the secretary shall be placed on top of the individual papers and neatly stapled at the left hand corner. The secretary will sign his or her name below the description.

- Team project outline to be followed:

a) DESCRIPTION: What is the business idea? What is its purpose? The short and long-term goals? Type of product or service that is to be offered to the public? Where will the business venture be located?

b) MARKETING: This is a plan that takes into consideration the product or service to be offered. Discuss the product's price. Its promotional concepts.

c) OUTSIDE SOURCES: What forms of assistance will be needed to get the venture off the ground? Examples: law offices, banks, advertising agencies. Why were these sources secured?

d) SECUREMENT AND USE OF CAPITAL: Anticipated organization of the business. How will the business operate? Who takes responsibility for what? Billing and collection procedures? Need for a computer system? Sales personnel?

In addition, the teacher has still other lesson techniques of student interest at his/her disposal. It is to these we next turn our attention.

"What I knew before"... lesson. A format that works well, and that can be adapted to any subject discipline, is the "what I knew before, what I now know, and what I've learned" lesson. With this format the teacher has class members divide a sheet of paper into three columns [lines can be drawn instead of folds] after placing the lesson number and Aim upon the chalkboard. This sheet becomes the lesson's motivational device. At the head of each column the student is asked to write the headings "What I Knew Before," "What I Now Know" and "What I've Learned." To save time the teacher might consider preparing class copies, of such a sheet, for distribution. Based upon the lesson for the day and/or using texts, source materials, graphic illustrations or the like, the instructor asks the class to tell what they presently know about a topic or subject to be discussed in class. Students are asked to record their thoughts in the first column. Discussion of student responses follow briefly. Instructions are then given to the class, by the teacher, to read or review the information source that has been made available to them.

After reading or reviewing the information source, students are asked to list their findings under the second column "What I Now Know." Classroom discussion continues once again. The third column is then used to summarize the lesson. This portion of the lesson is directed by the teacher, and student responses are summarized upon the chalkboard. The youngsters then copy the board summary onto the third column of their sheets.

Visual and audio aids. Most schools today have television monitors, VCR recorders and a wide selection of video tapes for adaptation to classroom use. Teachers can make excellent use of these materials for in-class learning experiences. A lesson that involves video viewing, or listening to a tape recording, requires special preparation by the teacher. A teacher contemplating using this type of lesson should keep the following in mind:

1. Preview the selection being considered for class use.

2. Be sure the selection meets the needs of subject content.

3. Take notes and develop questions you wish your youngsters to consider as they view the film. Be sure to note the appropriate frame number on the VCR where you might wish to pause in class for the purpose of having a discussion session.

4. TV and VCR usage serve only as an extended motivational device in most situations. The usual lesson components are followed. The viewing selection is not a substitute for the lesson itself.

The video lesson is always motivated prior to the tape's showing. The class is made aware that the film to be viewed correlates with the material content being taught in class. To save class time, the teacher prepares handouts. The handout has a lesson number with an "Aim" at the top. Below the Aim is a listing of several key vocabulary words, along with their definitions, which will be heard during the viewing. In addition, the handout contains three or four pivotal questions, with adequate space left beneath for students to record their observations. Because the teacher has previewed the film, he/she is able to stop its showing at preselected frames to conduct classroom discussion. Select video sections are used to reinforce previous classroom lessons or to set the stage for new ones. It is important to remember that a predetermined teacher time frame is established for a video lesson. Time, too, must be allocated for the necessary video lesson summary.

Primary and secondary sources. The use of original or secondary source materials also has a role in the classroom when offering a variety of lesson types. Such a lesson follows the usual format in procedure and development except that now the motivational device is a document or reading selection that meets a specific content need. The instructor prepares a handout of the selection to be used in class, once again. Important vocabulary words and their definitions head the sheet. The handout may be read aloud in class by the teacher and important concepts highlighted under his or her tutelage. Key concepts are summarized upon the chalkboard under appropriate headings. Pivotal questions are then asked which connect the reading selection to the subject content under study. This is followed by a final summary.

The school library lesson. The school library is a valuable research center for classroom projects and special assignments. The teacher is advised to familiarize his/her youngsters with its use by planning several library lessons during a term. In preparation for a library lesson, the subject teacher coordinates class activities with the school librarian. Generally, the librarian will want to know specifics such as the period for the lesson, the date and the lesson's objectives. The teacher plans this information so that the librarian, in turn, may prepare suitable resource materials for a class demonstration and/or an assignment. Cooperative planning between the teacher and the librarian helps to assure the lesson's success.

The subject teacher informs the youngsters of the pending library period and provides them with instructions as to the period, date and meeting place for the library session. On the day of the library lesson, the subject teacher posts a reminder upon the classroom door for latecomers and previous absentees if they are to meet initially in the library instead of the classroom. Depending upon the objectives of the library lesson, the teacher prepares his/her motivational sheet for distribution. The sheet has a lesson number, an Aim and a motivational device. It is also advised to write the homework assignment [if there is to be one] on this sheet, too. The instructor, depending upon the arrangements made with the librarian, might prepare a series of preliminary questions beneath the motivation or an outline of topics that will be discussed during the period. This should be done especially if one's school library has limited chalkboard use.

The computer room lesson. In this modern techno-logical age, teachers have the additional responsibility in preparing young people with computer competency. It is vitally important that students become computer literate in preparation for "the world of work." Most secondary schools, today, are equipped with computers that are available for student use; a computer-literate teacher or specialist is usually assigned as the school-wide instructor.

No matter what a teacher's academic discipline might be, a portion of the course work should be planned for the incorporation of computer instruction into the subject curriculum. Following a procedure similar to that of the library lesson the subject teacher plans, with assistance from the computer room instructor, a series of lessons that will uplift student skills. There are many excellent programs available for school use that meet the needs of specific subject areas. By mutually planning an agenda suitable to a specific need, young-sters can achieve great benefit from their computer room experiences.

Pre-test review lesson. This lesson, used for reviewing subject content prior to a quiz or test, need not be fraught with monotonous routine. A review lesson can be channeled into one of enjoyable classroom fun. The teacher need only use his/her imagination to make this lesson into a rewarding student experience.

The teacher initiates interest by informing students to study for an upcoming exam and that a specific day has been set aside for an in-class review. One way of stimulating interest is to turn the review lesson into a game or contest. The teacher may achieve this by dividing his/her class into two competitive teams. The teams stand on opposite sides of the classroom, facing each other. This is similar to the traditional spelling-bee arrangement used in elementary schools. Once this is done, the teacher becomes a classroom inquisitor of subject content. Students unable to answer the teacher's question, are told to quickly take their seats. The two remaining students, one from each team, are rewarded with a prize. One excellent motivation is to award bonus points toward the upcoming exam. This is particularly effective, and is well received by students. In addition, the teacher might want to inform the class of a pending prize before beginning the review lesson. Student awareness of a reward tends to heighten class enthusiasm for the lesson.

Another type of review lesson has the instructor write the name of an up-coming test topic or concept upon the chalkboard. A rectangle is framed around the written topic. In a chemistry class, for example, the teacher might select to write the word "atom" within a small rectangle. At the sides of the rectangle, small leg-like chalk lines are drawn. Students are asked to suggest whatever associations come to mind for the term "atom." Each student's suggestion, if correct, is written next to an attached leg of the rectangle. After student suggestions have been exhausted, the teacher asks for a definition of each item tagged to the rectangle-leg and for its relationship to the term "atom." Once a topic has been adequately covered the teacher erases the chalkboard, or the overhead transparency if that has been used, and initiates a new review topic. A teacher devised time frame is followed for both the board work and the question and answer periods.

Chapter Seven

TEACHING ACROSS-THE-CURRICULUM

Why teach across-the-curriculum? The teacher does not teach his/her discipline divorced from other academic areas. Students must be taught that knowledge is not divided into neat and isolated components. Rather, youngsters are to be prepared for the discovery that all subject areas share an interrelationship with one another and that such relationships are not pre-set by narrow or limited academic boundaries. How then might a subject teacher instruct students across the curriculum horizon while remaining within the parameters of his/her subject area?

All teachers should devote considerable time to reinforcing the language arts! The nation's schools should demand that students be able to communicate the English language with skill in reading, writing and speaking. Good writing is good thinking and secondary school teachers should be encouraged to enhance communicative expression by assigning frequent writing components, in addition to those of reading and speaking, into their classroom lessons.

Incorporating the language arts. As a case-in-point, assume that you are a health education teacher who has recently completed a unit on human nutrition. You wish your students to compile their notes and/or written homework centering upon a single component of a unit taught and then have them make use of their organizational and writing skills. Such a scenario invites an incorporation of the language arts into the health education environment. The teacher now orchestrates a "journey" across the curriculum of which the following is merely one way of proceeding.

A lesson for the writing of a business letter. Prepare a review lesson for the writing of a business letter. The lesson's Aim could be posed by the question, "How do we write an informative business letter?" A motivational statement, "Can you recall the components of a business letter?" relates to students' previous school experiences. After attending to basics [attendance taking, assigning homework upon the front chalkboard, and collecting the previous night's homework, if there was any], the teacher distributes unlined writing paper [8 1/2" x 11"] to each student. He/she then constructs a vertical rectangle [upon the front board] about three-quarters of a chalkboard slate.

The teacher informs the youngsters that "the chalkboard rectangle represents my sheet of writing paper." The instructor further explains that "I will demonstrate the margin dimensions, usually a constant, when writing a business letter. Copy these margin dimensions into your notebooks so that you can use them with a computer or word processor at a future date." Explain that margins are generally set 1 inch from both the top and bottom of the page and that the left margin is 1 inch from the outer edge, while the right margin is

1/2 inch from the edge of the paper. The teacher draws and labels these dimensions upon the chalkboard model. This operation can also be demonstrated using transparencies with an overhead projector. Next, tell the class that "there is an imaginary line that runs down the center of the page that is used as a guide for structuring the letter."

Restate the motivational question posed upon the front chalkboard. Once the teacher has reviewed the basic components of the business letter with the class, he/she writes the name of a fictitious letter-writer, the address and other relevant information at the side of the board rectangle. The teacher also writes the particulars for a person or company to whom the letter is being written. The instructor now reviews and completes the letter model with assistance from class members.

Begin by asking, "What do you think is the very first item that I should write upon my chalkboard model?" Anticipate considerable class interest [and many incorrect responses to the question]. After students have identified the appropriate line item, and its correct location, insert the item upon the chalkboard model. Continue this procedure of querying the youngsters for correct responses as to what should next be written upon the board model. The classroom aura created is generally one of stability and calm while the lesson's tone becomes that of an educational game. Student enthusiasm is maintained throughout the period's duration. When completed, the business letter model resembles Illustration #3. The teacher need not be concerned with completing the body of the letter. Instead, he/she should discuss content writing technique. Patiently explain, as well as outline on the chalkboard, the necessary "ingredients" for a readable and logically written paragraph.

The instructor should periodically reinforce what has been taught in this letter-writing exercise by having students frequently complete written assignments using the aforementioned format. This can be done regardless of the instructor's academic specialty.

Assign a letter-writing exercise in-class. Students first prepare a rough draft of their letters. They are told to correct for grammar, spelling and subject content. Upon completion, the youngsters pass their papers to designated classmates who, in turn, correct for English usage and subject content. The letters are then rewritten, finalized and submitted the next day, to the teacher, for a grade [can be considered as a short quiz worth up to 10 points in value].

2347 Rose Avenue
Atlanta, Georgia 34567
November 24, 1996

Mr. Jonathan Williams
J. M. Knowles & Company
1234 Benson Drive
Rome, New York 67891

Dear Mr. Williams:

[Content or body of letter begins here.]

Sincerely yours,

Rosalie Drummond

Illustration #3

An across-the-curriculum assignment. Inform students they will have an opportunity to earn 10 maximum bonus points that can be applied toward their end-of-term evaluation. Such an announcement is usually well received and acts as a positive motivation for the teacher's continuing, in-class or at-home, writing assignment. Instruct the class that each student is to write a business letter of 4 to 5 well-written paragraphs discussing the material they have learned, for example, concerning the physiological importance of vitamins upon humans. This assignment may also be continued the next day in class or designated as an additional homework to be completed over the next several days. Should the instructor decide that the assignment is to be done within the confines of the classroom, he/she now assumes the role of a language arts tutor. Students are made to feel free in calling upon the teacher for both writing and content assistance as he/she moves about the classroom. Ideally, the instructor should make the attempt to comment briefly upon, at minimum, one written paragraph per youngster. However brief, this lesson permits the teacher to offer hands-on instruction [particularly in classrooms of urban secondary schools with large student populations].

Across-the-curriculum lessons are not merely conducive to one or two academic disciplines. Easily, a math teacher can make the mathematical equation $F=ma$, for example, "come alive" by using it to explore the scientific world of physics and chemistry. Letter writing could be incorporated to enable youngsters to link the meaning of a variety of mathematical expressions with the physical sciences. Art, music, physical education, and foreign language teachers can similarly "cross over" into a variety of academic disciplines without difficulty. Teachers need only use their imaginations and creative skills!

Teaching a core curriculum. Teachers occasionally find themselves under the domain of "stale" and less than innovative subject-area supervisors. When a teacher desires to experiment with new classroom learning experiences, that may require supervisory approval, approach the supervisor enthusiastically with the proposal. If it is "sound" and "safe," most supervisors will permit the teacher to undertake the experiment even if they might not share the instructor's optimism. Secure the supervisor's expertise in fine-tuning the experiment. He/she can be administratively helpful in coordinating the logistics of a new instructional approach for the classroom.

Core instruction may be defined as a cooperative teaching venture involving two or more different subject teachers who integrate and link their subject disciplines into a single course. It is an additional example of classroom creativity to be considered as a teacher matures professionally. The positive results of cooperating ventures often have the dual effect of uplifting both teacher-supervisor morale and the level of student instruction. Core instruction, therefore, should be considered as a valuable teaching tool for classroom implementation.

Launching a cooperative core operation. Assume that a teacher of the language arts succeeds in getting his/her supervisor to approve a core studies arrangement with a social studies "buddy" teacher and the supervisor of the Social Studies Department. Both supervisors agree to give their administrative and supervisory assistance to the project. They proceed in arranging special school-programming for the joint-effort. Both instructors are given a program with two periods of core instruction each day while their other teaching assignments remain unaltered. Both the language arts and social studies teachers share the same class of youngsters for two core periods. The social studies teacher, for example, meets the class during period 3, while the other instructor meets the same class during period 4. Each instructor becomes the subject leader of his or her particular period assignment. However, each acts as a classroom "buddy" when he/she is not the primary subject teacher. Together the cooperating instructors plan a course-of-study in conjunction with their respective department supervisors. All parties to the project are cognizant of State mandated requirements when framing a new and experimental core teaching curriculum.

When not the primary teacher of the cooperative assignment, the buddy-teacher is free to grade papers, quizzes, and/or homework. The buddy is also available to tutor youngsters in his or her subject area as lesson planning permits. He is both a partner and an aide specialist to the primary teacher. The buddy-teacher remains with the class for the duration of an assigned period. This core operation permits a language arts teacher to offer his/her expertise to complement the social studies curriculum. Together, both academic subjects "gel" into a new unified whole offering students a greater opportunity to read and write across-the-curriculum. At the end of a term, each teacher remains responsible for entering an appropriate grade [the result of the end-of-term evaluation] for his/her subject discipline. Upon a term's completion, the experiment is evaluated for strengths, weaknesses and unforeseen problems. The core's evaluation should be undertaken in consultation with both the involved teachers and the appropriate supervisory personnel.

A teacher stimulates student creativity!

Chapter Eight

TEACHING SOCIAL VALUES

Classroom teachers have the responsibility of preparing youngsters for citizenship. They are the role models of good citizens and the advocates of positive social action. Each teacher's value system is an integral part of daily classroom activity.

Primary social value objectives. Classroom lessons in social values are based upon four broad primary objectives. They are:

1. respect for others
2. respect for self
3. respect for the natural environment
4. civic responsibility

These objectives permit the teacher avenues for both the exploration of ideas and experimentation with innovative approaches to instruction. The instructor sets an example for acceptable social behavior and prepares students for positive human-interaction. The teacher exemplifies the image of a peace-maker and a seeker-of-truth. He/she instructs youngsters in the processes of critical inquiry, analysis and problem-solving. Young people are also taught to be tolerant of one another.

Launching the value's lesson. During the early weeks of a new term, the teacher introduces the first of several value's lessons. A teacher-list of important social values is prepared for class distribution. This value's lesson, too, has both an Aim and a lesson number. The distributed class-sheet list is the lesson's motivation. Together, the teacher and class volunteers take turns reading aloud from the sheet. Students are asked to express their feelings and opinions during the give-and-take classroom discussion that follows. They are also encouraged to relate personal experiences to the discussion. As the lesson develops, additional social values noted by students and/or the teacher is written upon the chalkboard. The youngsters are asked to copy them onto their sheets along with the lesson's medial and final summary.

What follows is a partial list of themes [in no special order] that a teacher might consider developing for his/her value's lessons:

Social Values for Citizenship and Human Interaction

- Always give 100 % of yourself.
- Weigh options before making decisions.
- Do not allow emotions to rule one's brain. Think before taking action!
- Show respect for all people.
- Do not delay for tomorrow, what you can do today.
- Injustice for one is injustice for all!

- Do not flee from a problem. Confront it head-on!
- Learn to distinguish fact from opinion.
- Demonstrate self-confidence. Learn to accept criticism.
- Live and let live. Be tolerant of others.
- If you make a fool of yourself, be prepared to pay the consequences.
- Do not gossip!
- Failure usually precedes success.
- Struggle so that you may win.
- Do not scapegoat others for faults that are your own.
- You may not agree with others but show respect for their opinions.
- In a democracy, a lack of respect for law and order moves us closer to the law of the jungle.
- Do your part in maintaining a clean environment so that all may live healthy lives.

The teacher may wish to use newspapers, magazines, short stories and novels to supplement the VCR, television and radio in future value's lessons. Class-trips to government and private institutions can also be undertaken. In addition, guest-speakers from the community can be brought into the classroom to speak about civic responsibility.

Secondary social value objectives. In the preparation of value's lessons, the teacher has at his/her disposal important secondary objectives which can be used as a guide in formulating a variety of lesson plans for class instruction. What follows is a list of several secondary social value objectives:

- Students will understand ethical questions to be part of everyday life.
- Students will be able to distinguish what is right from what is wrong.

- Students will acquire a "sense of justice."
- Students will learn to find personal answers to ethical questions.
- Students will discover that there are customs that regulate how people behave toward one another.
- Students will understand that a moral code is the foundation of society and if it is broken punishment will follow.
- Students will gain respect for themselves, others and the community in which they live.

Abridged models for social value lessons. What follows are two abridged models or themes to guide the teacher in preparing future value's lessons for his/her class.

Model I

Aim: Why is it important to be courteous?

Objective: Students will identify 3 potential consequences resulting from a lack of courtesy in a series of common situations.

Questions: How would you define the term courtesy?
In your opinion, how can courtesy toward others
help you "get ahead" in the world?
In your opinion, how can courtesy toward others
defuse situations that breed anger and ill-will?

Possible activities:
- Have students break into groups to write role-plays based upon assigned scenarios. These scenarios might be related to job interviews, parental confrontations, and teacher-student conflicts.
- Have students "improvise" role-plays based upon the above-noted scenarios.

Model II

Aim: How do we determine the difference between objective news reporting and editorializing?

Objective: Students will examine media terminology and identify 3 biases in some commonly used phrases.

Questions: What is meant by the phrase "objective reporting?"
In your opinion, what are the necessary ingredients for objective reporting?
How do we determine reporting that is not objective?

Possible Activities:

- Review the functions and effects of modifiers.
- Read newspaper articles and view videos of news reports isolating modifying words and phrases which "color" the reports.
- Compile a list of commonly used phrases that tend to skew the objectivity of news reporting.
- Rewrite news articles, replacing slanted with objective terminology.

Value's instruction present a teaching opportunity for having students read, speak and write about ethical and social issues. It is suggested that the instructor's activities place emphasis upon student expression that use speaking and writing pathways. The teacher's assignments should also include investigative techniques that make use of questionnaires and interviews. Co-op learning and role playing lessons should be carefully planned so that youngsters accept them enthusiastically. At the discretion of the instructor, grades for value's projects could be based upon both student creativity and growth in oral and written expression.

A teacher is firm but fair to all.

Chapter Nine

TESTING

Remember how we hated to take tests as youngsters? Our stomachs echoed familiar sounds and our psyches gravitated toward mild, but temporary, depression when our teachers announced that, "next week we'll have an exam." What upset us was that such an announcement meant we were no longer totally free over the next several days to conduct "business as usual." A test announcement meant one thing- that the burden of test preparation was once again upon us! A teacher can empathize with youngsters when a familiar group moan is heard upon the announcement of an impending exam.

The classroom test. The classroom test is an important component of the learning environment. It is by no means a total measure of what the student has learned. It is, however, an indicator of a student's progress in learning the content material expected of him or her. With this in mind it is important that the teacher understand the necessity for good test design; a test should measure what it is intended to measure! This is vital for the preparation of a valid test. A well written test is an indicator of what students have or have not learned. It also aids the instructor in discovering which unit objectives were or were not achieved.

Similarly, a good test is reliable in that it is consistent in its measurement and is clearly defined in its objective. The teacher wishes to avoid test design which places emphasis on insignificant content material, makes use of vague questions, and causes confusion in grading. One cannot test all content covered both in and outside of the classroom. Know what you want to test! Is the exam designed to reveal particular strengths or weaknesses? Is the teacher seeking insight with regard to student mastery or minimum competency of content learned? Does its design penalize the slower student or those with reading disabilities?

Test design. There are a variety of test formats the teacher can use as a basis for achieving good test design. Some, but not all, are listed:

1. The multiple-choice test
2. The true-false test
3. The matching test
4. The completion or fill-in test
5. The essay test
6. The oral presentation test
7. The case study test

In addition, the teacher has a choice of selecting the site where a test is to be administered, either in-class or at home. More about these options shortly.

The multiple-choice, true or false, matching, and completion tests are all objective exam formats. As such they all offer advantages as well as problems. Their positive features are that exam answers are either right or wrong and are easy to mark. The problems they pose are more complex. When such formats are used, the teacher can easily offer an uneven sampling of test items, which in turn produce an unequal weighting for the exam as a whole. Further, a strong case can be made for the argument that inadequate critical thinking takes place when answering objective test items; emphasis is placed primarily upon student ability to memorize content material.

Other test formats listed previously are subjective types. These types, although having theoretical limitations of their own, are more advantageous than objective tests. They call upon students to demonstrate multiple-skills that they have acquired, thereby enabling them to be more critical in their thinking.

The oral presentation test is undertaken when the teacher desires to evaluate an individual's ability to communicate information to others. It examines a youngster's ability to understand cause and effect relationships and to then clearly present conclusions before the class and instructor.

The case study or discovery test asks the student to investigate something unfamiliar. For example, the teacher might direct classroom members to go to a local museum. Students are provided with a set of teacher-directed questions to be answered as when viewing a particular exhibit relative to class study. The youngsters are then required, at a later date, to evaluate their observations either orally or written.

The teacher sets learning goals for both the individual student and the class as a whole. He/she tests to measure individual achievement and class success. The test becomes an indicator of progress being made. Many teachers initiate testing procedures of habit. Their routine consists of announcing an exam several days before it is administered. The class is told which lessons and text pages to study. On "test day" the youngsters are administered the exam that they complete within a specified time frame.

The teacher should consider altering both the routine and administration of the classroom test. Many teachers do not quiz frequently enough. As a result, students are required to spend considerable time in rote-memorization of notes and homework in preparation for test day. For many young people this is often a difficult task tending to favor those with retention ability and no learning disabilities while handicapping others who may be less academically inclined. Generally, rote-memorization of notes is a hinderance to critical thinking when preparing for a test.

Alternative testing methods. Thirty-three years of personal teaching experience has demonstrated that there are other methods for conducting class tests. For example, at the end of each school week give students a short subjective quiz that covers both the week's classroom content and homework. Alternate these quizzes in style. Upon one occasion the teacher might give a written multiple-choice, true or false or fill-in test consisting ten questions to be completed in seven or eight minutes. On an other occasion test questions could be read to the class aloud by the instructor. Students record their answers upon pre-distributed blank quiz papers. In such an arrangement the teacher informs the class that each question will be read twice and that they should listen attentively before they write their answers next to the appropriate question number. This testing format calls upon youngsters to adopt good listening habits so that they may learn to respond to oral questioning in the future. After administering an oral quiz, permit 15-20 seconds for the class to review their answer choices. Once this is completed the quiz is graded in-class by the students.

Students grading tests. Youngsters love to grade papers. They also wish to know their test grades as quickly as possible. Having the class grade a quiz, therefore, serves a dual purpose with an added bonus that the teacher is "rescued" from the task of grading twenty-five to thirty short quiz papers. Pursue this procedure in the following manner:

After announcing that "the quiz is over- put down all pens," have the last students in each row stand. Tell them to bring their test paper to the person sitting in the first seat of their row, to place it upon that desk and to then return to their seats. Next, inform the rest of the class to pass their papers back one seat. Each student now signs his/her name at the bottom of the test paper. He/she now becomes an official grader and is responsible for correctly marking the quiz. In addition, explain that "if there are any unusual or unexplained discrepancies in a student's quiz grade upon the return of the papers, one or two points will be deducted from the student who graded the quiz."

The teacher now gives instruction to the class as to how grading is done. He/she says, "I will read each question, which will then be followed by a student's answer to that question. If I state that an answer is correct, you will place no mark on the paper. If the student answer is incorrect, you will place an X next to the number. If there are any blank spaces next to a question number, you are to place a circle with a line through it and then mark an X next to its number." This explanation is followed by the teacher reading the quiz questions and class members offering answers to the questions. When grading is completed, tell the students that each correct answer has a value of one point. They are then to place the correct score neatly at the top of the paper with a circle around it. Papers are then collected. Students receiving a grade of six or higher are verbally informed of it by the teacher, who reads the score aloud. A failing score is read only if a youngster requests it. The teacher records the scores at a later time into his/her grading book and returns the quizzes, usually, by the next class meeting. The entire procedure takes no longer than twenty minutes. For the remainder of the class period, the instructor completes the previous lesson, if left undone, or initiates the introduction of a new one.

Changing the essay test format.
The so-called full-period test can also be altered in style to meet student needs. Assume a language arts, science or social studies teacher desires to offer an essay exam during a typical forty-minute period. He/she has completed a particular unit of study and now wishes to subjectively test the youngsters. The teacher desires to know if students have mastered unit concepts and if they can describe acquired information in an organized and documented manner.

Prepare a class test sheet with from one-to-three essays, which will be distributed to the class approximately one week before an in-class exam. At the top of these papers are teacher directions to be followed. The essay test questions should be brief and clear in meaning. Distribute a test sheet to each student. Inform the youngsters that they may prepare their essays at home. They may use their text, class notes, and any additional sources to write their first few drafts and the final copy. Essay answers should be well organized, events, names and dates clearly defined, and the written work carefully checked for good English usage. When this has been done, and they are satisfied with their work, they are to put final copy answers to memory. In a week's time they will be given an opportunity to recreate their essay answers, from memory, in-class. However, the teacher will select either one-of-two or one-of-three essays to answer the day of the exam. Students are pre-informed that the teacher will select *only one* essay to be answered. This same process can be followed for a variety of essay tests. In addition, the teacher has the choice of giving a take-home essay exam without testing in-class. In this scenario, a draft is first submitted by the student to the teacher. The draft is reviewed with written recommendations and returned to the youngster. The final copy, accompanied by the original teacher-corrected draft, is then submitted at a specified date for a grade.

Illustration #4 is an sample of a take-home test in which the teacher assists youngsters in finding information for completing an exam:

Biology II   Name_____
John Smith, Teacher
Test #3

This is a take-home exam once again. However, this time **you do not have to memorize your essay answers.** You should first prepare **an outline answer to all three parts below and then combine them into one unified essay.** Your test will be graded for both content and English usage. This exam is due no later than *November 12, 1996.* I have given you some assistance by numbering the pages in your textbook where you can find additional information to supplement classroom notes.

A.   State Jean Baptiste de Lamarck's Theory of Evolution. (262-64)
B.   Discuss how 18th century biologists prepared the way for our understanding of evolutionary change. Be sure to discuss the contributions of the following: (270-72)
      1. August Weismann
      2. Charles Darwin
C.   How did genetic principles, discovered in the 20th century, modify Darwin's theory of natural selection? (286-88)

Illustration #4

The teacher is a classroom leader.

Chapter Ten

THE END-OF-TERM EVALUATION

A teacher should be firm but fair. Teacher "fairness" becomes a crucial factor in evaluating student performance as the term approaches its climax. The teacher is reminded of a need for awareness of individual differences among youngsters. Failing students deserve some last opportunity to reverse a failing term performance. Can this be done, however, without totally invalidating a student's past performance? Experience demonstrates that this is indeed possible.

Comprehensive exams. About one month before the completion of the term, announce that there will be an opportunity for failing students to still pass your class. A comprehensive in-class exam will be given to all class members over a two-day period. This exam will cover the entire term's course work. The test will be both objective and subjective in format. Further, explain that the comprehensive offers something positive for all students. Those who are presently failing will have the opportunity to still pass the class provided that they secure a passing score. However, such youngsters will not receive a final term grade greater than a minimum 65. They must obtain a 65 on the comprehensive exam in order to convert their present failing grade to a passing one. Those students who are presently passing the course are rewarded with an additional 5 points for the term grade if they in-turn receive a 65 or greater on the exam. Thus, a student presently with an 80 average who secures a 65 or better on the comprehensive will be eligible for an 85. So that youngsters know exactly where they presently stand with regard to grade performance, the teacher updates and informs each student of his/her present performance as the class enters the final month of the term. To do this, the teacher sets aside a class period from actual instruction. It is not necessary to assign a class-project during this period, for students are too excited to concentrate upon it. Students are permitted to talk quietly to each other. However, the teacher is free to select options that meet his/her class needs.

At the instructor's desk, he/she reads to each student [from the teacher's grade book] the following: quizzes, tests, midterm [a double score] and reports and/or special class grades. This is followed by a reading of missing homework [excluding the three permitted as announced at the beginning of the term] and assigned demerit points. As the teacher reads, each youngster copies his/her term scores onto a sheet of paper. The teacher informs the class that talking volume is to be held to a minimum during the grade readings. Youngsters are generally very cooperative and well behaved during this session. They should, however, be reminded that the teacher's review of class performance is done as a courtesy, and that if abused the process will be discontinued.

After a student has been informed of his/her updated performance status, each summates the points and deducts five points for each missing homework and each demerit. This final tally represents the points earned for the term. Students are told to keep their statements safe for the final student-teacher interview at the end of the term. Any additional quizzes, tests, missing homework and demerits, which may still be given during the remaining month, will be added and/or subtracted from the score already earned. After all the youngsters have been informed of their academic performance and the teacher has entered each students total points [in pencil] into his record book, the teacher then calculates, in full view of all students, the value of the course upon the chalkboard [see Chapter One for a review of the procedure]. Each student quickly discovers whether he/she is presently passing or failing the course. For some youngsters, the end-of-term comprehensive exam now becomes a crucial final opportunity to pass the class.

Preparing students for the comprehensive exam.

A constant and on-going problem confronting the classroom teacher is how best to serve all youngsters in spite of the gamut of differences in academic ability. This is of particular concern to the teacher as the end of a term approaches and there are students who are on the verge of failure. What, in all fairness, can a teacher do that would permit each youngster a last opportunity to pass the class or improve upon his/her grade?

Several weeks before the end of the term, and after the teacher has informed the youngsters of their academic standing in the class, notify the students that you are setting aside time for comprehensive exam review. The teachers prepare a series of self-study in-class review sheets that cover the term's content. A review sheet is distributed every other day for individualized in-class instruction. Each assignment has a series of primary and pivotal questions with appropriate lines drawn beneath the questions for youngsters to write their summary answers. Text books, classnotes and any other necessary materials are permitted for use. Students have the option of working together in small groups or by themselves. The classroom instructor provides each student with a legal size manila-folder [these can be secured from the Department Chairperson]. Students are informed to write their names upon them and that they are to maintain them for all pre-comprehensive review work.

The teacher's function during the review sessions is to act as a resource person. Students are informed that "I [the teacher] am available to help you if you should need my assistance with the review material. Just raise your hand and I will come to your seat." The teacher, in this way, creates an atmosphere that offers both comfort and security. This is always appreciated by those young people who need the teacher's assistance and encouragement the most.

Deadlines are established for the completion of each review sheet. Those students who have not completed the task in a given time frame are permitted to do so as part of their regular homework assignment. In addition to collecting the term's remaining homework assignments each day, the instructor collects 4-5 classroom folders each day for spot checking. A teacher-memo, evaluating a student's review work, is inserted into his/her folder. These are returned the next day. Folders may be taken home for study but only after a student has made his/her request known to the teacher and has signed the teacher-created "take-home sheet." The results of a short quiz each week, during the review period, acts as a barometer that indicates how well a youngster has been preparing for the comprehensive exam.

At the appropriate time for a final exam, as determined by the school calendar, the teacher administers the comprehensive examination to the class. Exams are graded and the results quickly reported back to students before the last few classes of the term. The stage is now set for the final student-teacher interviews.

Student-teacher rapport is a key to learning!

Student-teacher interviews. The instructor announces the day that he/she will hold interviews to finalize student grades. Remember that interviews are held after the comprehensive exam results have been returned to students. At these interviews the teacher discusses, with the student, the merits of his/her term's performance. Students are reminded that those who are failing should not request a 75 or an 80, for it will not be granted. They are, however, encouraged to be open and frank about personal feelings and perceptions regarding their performance. The student is given an opportunity for self-evaluation and input. Any discussion between teacher and student is done in an environment of mutual "give and take."

At the start of the teacher-student interview, the instructor first cross-checks the the student's statement of total points earned with those in the class record book. The student is asked to suggest the grade he/she believes has been earned based upon the point system. In those cases where the total points earned fall between two scores [for example between 75 and 80] the teacher and the student, together, seek to reach agreement based upon the individual's overall effort. As a result of the discussion, the lower or higher score becomes the assigned final grade. The teacher remains, however, the final evaluator of the course grade if no agreement is reached.

A teacher instructs youngsters in positive social values.

A teacher assists students to succeed in the classroom.

Chapter Eleven

CLASSROOM DISCIPLINE AND GUIDANCE

A teacher cannot teach unless his/her classroom is orderly. The task of maintaining discipline, and it is often a difficult one, is initially the responsibility of the instructor. For the novice teacher, keeping a class disciplined is frequently a monumental endeavor. The contents of this book are specifically designed within the scope of preventive discipline. As such, it is of considerable assistance to the beginning or relatively new teaching professional.

Teacher as a role model. A teacher must have genuine concern for the young people who enter his/her classroom. Having been a "kid," the teacher has some understanding of adolescents and the problems and fears youngsters confront daily. As a role model, the teacher demonstrates both courtesy and consideration to those under his/her charge. In addition, the teacher demonstrates maturity and self-control in dealing with class and individual problems as well as special situations when they arise. The teacher is charged with the burden of creating an environment that instills security, sharing and a sense of togetherness. Teacher preparation and planning, effective management and organization are all necessary ingredients for the maintenance and continuity of good classroom discipline.

Discipline and guidance. The teacher should be aware of the differences between discipline and guidance needs. Even the typical socially well-adjusted youngster may, upon occasion, become a sudden discipline problem. The causes may be numerous. He/she may not be feeling well or may even have a serious problem at home that is a cause of personal unhappiness, discomfort or stress. On any given day a classmate and/or the teacher could be on the receiving end of such a youngster's agitated state-of-mind. However, young-sters who act out on an almost daily basis may be symptomatic of some personal and/or social maladjustment. The teacher should not be quick to place "labels" upon such youngsters. Rather, he/she should have a ready plan of action for the most typical forms of student misbehavior.

The teacher is expected to assert needed discipline within his/her classroom. He/she is indeed the first-line of defense in establishing classroom order. Only after a teacher's endeavors have failed to stabilize the classroom decorum, usually resulting from an unruly student or students, may he/she act in conjunction with the school's established "ladder of action" or "chain of discipline." This is not to say, however, that as an emergency arises, the teacher need act alone. Any situation that is beyond a teacher's immediate control, and/or which appears to endanger both the teacher and members of the class, requires that he/she call upon an available security guard, supervisor and/or administrator for assistance. Such immediate action may first be undertaken by opening the classroom door and securing a helping hand. If no one is available in the school corridor, a quickly written message to an administrator, carried by a reliable student monitor along with a classroom pass, should bring assistance.

The instructor should document all student infractions by citing the date, time, a description of the misbehavior and the disciplinary action taken including to whom referred and whether or not a parent was notified [see "Teacher Forms"].

Ordinary run-of-the-mill situations of students' acting-out usually require no more than a firm teacher command to "stop." The teacher can also change a student/students' seats for a class period when necessary. The instructor may request that a poorly behaved student meet with him/her after class to discuss the behavioral problem. At such a meeting the teacher stresses his/her "unhappiness" with the student's behavior while offering the youngster an opportunity to explain the reasons, if any, for acting out. In so doing, the teacher sets the stage for preventive discipline into the future. For students who exemplify atypical behavior, however, the instructor pursues a different avenue of approach. It is at this point that the guidance vehicle becomes a necessity.

Records. The instructor should carefully investigate student records before submitting a formal complaint to guidance personnel. Often, unruly behavior may be the result of student misplacement resulting from a programming error. A youngster, for example, who should have been placed in a normal mainstream rather than an honor or advanced placement class-setting, was inadvertently misprogrammed. Many times such students are unaware of an error in placement and, as a result of their discomfort, continually misbehave. At other times a young person may be suffering from a vision, hearing, or other handicap that has not been made known to the teacher. A careful check of both academic and health records could disclose a possible cause for a student's misbehavior.

Fact-finding. The teacher may, in addition, select to hold a fact-finding conference with a student and, when necessary, with both the student and his parent/parents to determine the cause of an existing discipline problem. At such a meeting a parent-teacher monitoring plan could be arranged that would keep the family informed of the youngster's progress. When initiating disciplinary action, the teacher is reminded to keep an ongoing record including dates, place of meetings and/or phone conversations. The teacher might also confer informally with other teachers, guidance personnel and/or supervisors who know the youngster in question with the intention of gaining greater insight into a behavioral problem. The instructor might further offer a repeating offender a special arrangement. For example, for every two or three days of good behavior, the teacher rewards the problem youngster with a bonus point creditable to the end of term grade. There are occasions where such an arrangement will work well in curtailing or eliminating unruly behavioral problems. After the teacher has acted upon the aforementioned remedies, and the problem continues to persist, the teacher then refers a youngster through the established chain of school guidance personnel.

Agencies-of-referral. Typically there are two basic school agencies-of-referral. The first and immediate agency is usually composed of a dean and an academic assistant principal. The dean's role is to handle immediate discipline problems as they arise and to then take preventive measures so that infractions are not repeated. The academic assistant principal acts upon all cases within his/her department which relate to instruction. Generally, this individual confers with youngsters who confront an immediate academic dilemma. For repeating and consistent offenders, where continuous counseling and follow-up become necessary, students are remanded to a second agency-of-referral. This agency is composed of guidance, health, attendance counselors and other related school personnel who deal with special situations. It is generally the principal's office that determines the merits of a suspension.

Chapter Twelve

EVALUATING A LESSON

Imagine you are an observer of Ms. Whitestone's science class in biology. What follows is a description of her classroom activities. Attempt to evaluate this fictitious instructor's performance listing both her teaching strengths and weaknesses.

Class: Biology 23
Period: Fourth, 10:40 A.M. to 11:20 A.M.
Class Level: average ability. Register: 32
Yesterday's lesson topic: Historical development of cell theory. Homework was assigned for the next day [Tuesday].

10:41: Ms. Whitestone begins by taking class attendance. There are seven students absent. Students are talking quietly with their neighbors. After three or four minutes, the teacher asks that everyone pass forward last night's homework to the first seat in their respective rows.

"Do homework number eight for tomorrow," she says. "We'll have a full period test some time next week. I'll let you know more on Thursday."

10:44: The following Aim is placed upon the chalkboard "Plant vs Animal Cells." Beneath the Aim, the teacher creates two columns. The first is headed "Plants" and the second column "Animals."

As she writes, a girl in the third seat second row calls out, "Can I go to the bathroom?"

Ms. Whitestone turns from the board and says, "Don't yell out, please! Wait until I finish." The teacher proceeds to complete her board-work and then collects homework from each of the front desks.

"The pass is on my desk, Mary. Come back quickly from the Girls' Room," remarks the teacher.

Mary stands, takes the pass, waves to a friend and leaves the room shutting the door behind her with a loud bang.

10:48: Ms. Whitestone continues.

"Renee, what did we study yesterday?"

Renee answers apathetically, "I don't remember."

The teacher continues. "John, tell us?"

John, startled at first, answers "Oh, about cell life and how they are part of all living things."

"Good!" replies Ms. Whitestone.

From the back of the room a student yells out, "It's hot in here. Can I open a window?"

"How many are warm?" asks the teacher. Nine hands are raised.

"O.K., I'll open a window from the top. I don't want anyone getting hurt." Ms. Whitestone opens the window.

10:55:   Mary returns from the Girls' Room, waves to a friend, returns the pass to the teacher's desk and takes her seat. Ms. Whitestone continues.

"Recalling last night's homework, can you describe one basic difference between plant and animal cells?" asks the teacher. Three hands are raised. Ms. Whitestone calls upon Phil.

"Plant cells have a cell wall?"

"Good!" replies the teacher. "Cynthia, what do you think?"

"Ms. Whitestone, I didn't have my hand up," remarks the girl rather sarcastically.

"I know that but I'm sure the class would be interested in your opinion," responds the teacher.

Mark yells out, "Animal cells don't have a cell wall."

"Excellent," replies the instructor. Ms. Whitestone goes to the blackboard and writes beneath the heading "Plants:"

"1. cell wall"

The teacher turns to the class once again.

"What else?" she asks.

11:01: There is silence. Ms. Whitestone turns to the chalkboard and continues the completion of her column:

"2. chloroplasts 3. large vacuoles"

The teacher creates a chalkboard drawing of a plant cell and lectures the class on the form and function of its structures. She tells the class to copy the board diagram into their notebooks as she walks to and then stands behind her desk.

11:15: "O.K. Now, let's turn our attention to animal cells," says the teacher. "In your opinion, how are animal cells different from plant cells? Who knows? Jimmy, what do you think?"

Jimmy answers, "I don't know, teacher." Alice raises her hand.

"Yes, Alice?"

"Ms. Whitestone, may I go to the Girls' Room?"

"Take the pass you know where it is," answers the teacher.

"Does anyone know?" asks Ms. Whitestone once again.

"Know what?" asks a boy in the fourth row third seat.

"The answer to my question," states Ms. Whitestone in obvious frustration.

"Can you repeat the question, please?" asks Peter.

11:18: Ms. Whitestone repeats the question but receives no response from the class.

"O.K., let's copy the board," says Ms. Whitestone as she picks up a piece of chalk once again.

Under the heading "Animals," she writes:

"1. no cell wall 2. centrioles 3. small vacuoles"

Alice returns from the Girls' Room, walks behind Ms. Whitestone, places the pass on the desk and returns to her seat. The bell rings ending the period.

"See you tomorrow. Have a nice day," says the teacher brushing off white chalk-dust from her blouse.

QUESTIONS FOR YOU TO CONSIDER

1. Does Ms. Whitestone demonstrate any strengths as a teacher? Explain.

2. Identify weaknesses in Ms. Whitestone's lesson with regard to the following instructional areas:
    a. classroom management
    b. launching the lesson
    c. lesson development
    d. questioning technique
    e. maintaining classroom order
    f. adequate use of the chalkboard
    g. lesson timing
    h. lesson summaries

3. If you were assisting Ms. Whitestone in improving her classroom performance, what would be your <u>most immediate</u> recommendation for change?

TURN TO PAGE 110 FOR AN EVALUATION OF THE LESSON

A teacher prepares students with the necessary skills

for problem solving.

A teacher inspires students to learn how they may help themselves.

AN EVALUATION OF MS. WHITESTONE'S LESSON

Ms. Whitestone appears to be a motivated classroom teacher but lacks basic understanding of classroom operations and solid teaching methodology. She has, however, demonstrated that she is familiar with the rudiments of the classroom operation as indicated by the following:

- She took the daily attendance as is generally required.
- The teacher assigned homework and collected the previous assignment. She gave notice of an upcoming exam.
- Ms. Whitestone placed an "Aim" upon the chalkboard.
- The teacher demonstrated an ability toward good questioning technique as when she asked, "Recalling last night's homework, can you describe one basic difference between plant and animal cells?" She personalized the question for the class with a reference to the previous night's homework and use of the pronoun "you."
- She was courteous to her students, which assures her chances for eventually securing greater student-teacher rapport.

However, Ms. Whitestone's weaknesses are typical of many new teachers to the secondary school classroom. The following weaknesses are noted:

The teacher demonstrated poor classroom management. She did not set priorities for those operations that are vital to classroom stability. Her "Aim" should have been elicited from the class and written upon the chalkboard as a question to be answered. An improved "Aim" for the lesson might have been, "What are the structural differences between plant and animal cells?" A motivation should have been placed either upon the chalkboard or another vehicle used such as a reading selection or a comparing plant and animal cell diagram-handout. The teacher's two column boardwork, headed "Plants" and "Animals," did not serve the class well as a motivational tool. In addition, Ms. Whitestone should have taken attendance as her class copied the front boards and concerned themselves with the motivational device. The teacher failed to bring her class to order and readiness.

The instructor should not have verbalized the homework assignment but rather written it upon the chalkboard in a designated homework position. By her verbalizing the assignment, students may have not heard it nor the occasional latecomer been aware of it. The homework should have been collected following attendance-taking. The announcement of a pending exam "sometime next week" would have been better served as a notation beneath the day's homework assignment.

Ms. Whitestone needed to establish clearly defined rules for the use of the pass in her classroom. Personal experience in the classroom demonstrates that it is best that the pass not be issued, the exception being an emergency, for the first and last ten minutes of a class-period. In addition, no more than three students should be allowed to leave the room during any one period. The pass should be placed at a strategic location at the front of the room so that a student may exit and re-enter with minimum disruption. Any student yelling out for the pass forfeits its use. Students should become conditioned to raising their hands if they wish to leave the room.

Ms. Whitestone failed to adequately develop her lesson. Seven minutes passed before Ms. Whitestone called upon Renee to undertake a summary of the previous day's work. The teacher also failed to initiate a review question, which would have launched her review session. It was at this point, to say the least, that the instructor lost the class. By often repeated requests, of different students, to answer a poorly phrased question and in her failure to rephrase it into a meaningful and understandable manner, Ms. Whitestone simply added to class confusion. Further, the instructor made no attempt to remedy the constant yelling out. She failed to direct class members to raise hands when trying to attract her attention. Ms. Whitestone clearly demonstrated her inability to lead!

One cannot teach until the teacher assumes his/her role of classroom leader. Discipline is a must! No teacher can proceed to teach without first establishing classroom discipline. If a class remains unruly, after a teacher's request for classroom order, the instructor should direct the class to close their notebooks. The lesson is over for the day! He/she erases the chalkboards, puts his/her lesson away, quickly assigns demerits into the student profile book, for those lacking discipline [later a telephone call should be made or a letter mailed to guardians], and directs the class to remain quiet until the end-of-the-period bell. The teacher, in a firm tone of voice, informs the students that this procedure will continue as often as may be necessary. When a lesson is so terminated, students are held accountable for the lesson's content. Experience has demonstrated that most students will exert peer pressure upon those who are unruly when the teacher is forced to repeatedly terminate lessons. However, the cause of Ms. Whitestone's problem was not directly related to a situation of unruly students but rather in her failure to implement good classroom operations and incorporate solid teaching technique!

Further, Mary's return to class at 10:55 A.M. should have been challenged by Ms. Whitestone [student was out of the room for 11 minutes] and the student told to speak with the teacher after class. Mary should be prohibited from using the pass until her guardians are notified of her behavior. Until then, Ms. Whitestone should request that Mary bring a letter from a urologist or family doctor explaining the need for a lavatory stay of 11 minutes before she is permitted the pass again. As a result of all the aforementioned, the teacher's lesson review did not occur.

Ms. Whitestone's lesson development was flawed by her questioning technique. She failed to ask the preliminary questions, which would have permitted the class to move into the more complex definitions of cell structure. As a result, she failed to both develop the lesson's factual content and to stimulate classroom interest. Had the teacher first asked the class to review the previous day's notes from their notebooks, Ms. Whitestone may well have succeeded in moving the lesson along. Lesson development failed to materialize because of a lack of classroom discussion, which should have moved from student-to-student to student-to-student and back to the teacher. To have each youngster contribute to classroom discussion is always the ideal. This will not occur, however, unless the teacher finds a means of making it happen!

Ms. Whitestone's chalkboard activity was self-imposed. Because of a lack of classroom socialization, her boardwork became the means of filling the classroom void. This, too, resulted in failure. The chalkboard outline never materialized in a way that added to the lesson's development. Rather, it was incomplete; it lacked clarity and cohesiveness. Her chalkboard responses were not placed under appropriate headings but written beneath oversimplified topic headings such as "Plants" and "Animals." Boardwork thus lacked a logical and understandable gathering of information and interpretation for students. There were no preliminary [medial] or final summaries. This further added to the lesson's lack of structure and order. In addition, Ms. Whitestone appeared to have lost all sense of class time. This, too, assured the lesson's failure.

A teacher motivates students to think critically.

Chapter Thirteen

CLASSROOM PROBLEMS

Below are a series of problems that might confront a teacher in the classroom. In the spaces provided, indicate your brief solution by writing what you would do for each classroom scenario.

1. During your lessons, students have repeatedly informed you that they do not understand many of your questions.

----

2. A student constantly yells out answers to your questions during recitation.

----

3. Students A and B, sitting in the back of the class, are talking and giggling.

----

4. A student participates actively during your classroom lessons and demonstrates an obvious grasp of the content material. However, he has a failing test average.

----

5. A female student suddenly faints in class.

----

6. You are administering a weekly quiz and suddenly there is an unannounced fire drill.

----

7. Twenty-three of twenty-seven students haved failed your midterm exam.

----

8. A student submits a neatly typed and bound book report for your acceptance two days after the pre-set deadline.

----

9. An irate parent calls to tell you her daughter deserves more than the grade of 85 you have given her for the term. She accuses you of

bias toward the student and informs you that she will see the principal about the matter if the grade is not changed.

----

10. You have recently noted there is an excessive amount of classroom cutting during your seventh period.

SEE PAGE 119 FOR "POSSIBLE SOLUTIONS TO

PROBLEMS"

The teacher is cognizant of individual differences.

POSSIBLE SOLUTIONS TO CLASSROOM PROBLEMS

1. Reevaluate your questioning technique. Are you speaking clearly and loudly enough so that you are heard from all points of the room? Ask several youngsters, who sit in the rear and to the sides of the room, whether your voice is being heard clearly. Review your lesson questions. Are they brief and to the point? Have you made use of the pronouns "you" and "we" to personalize questions and do they relate to student experiences? Have you avoided questions that can be answered with a single word or others that could be redundant?

2. Tell the student, so that all may hear, that you appreciate his enthusiasm but that you will not acknowledge his contribution unless he raises his hand. It is important that discussion occur in an orderly fashion so class-members can listen to others who are speaking. Ask the student to see you after class for a moment. Inform him/her at this meeting that there are bonus points available if he/she learns to control his/her outbursts. These bonus points [one or two value points of credit toward an exam grade] can be given at the end of the school week.

3. Tell students A and B that you're very unhappy with their lack of consideration for others in the class. Assign them both to other available seats for the lesson in question. Inform them that new seats will be made permanent if their misbehavior continues.

4. Obviously something is wrong. Ask the student to meet with you privately to discuss his test performance. At this meeting ask him for the possible cause of the problem. Listen carefully to his explanation. It may offer clues as to how you might assist him. If the response is vague, "dig" a bit further. Ask if the student knows how to study and prepare for an exam. Are there problems at home that hinder studying for an exam? Are there indications of physical problems that might explain the poor performance results? Based upon the

student's responses, make appropriate recommendations. If a serious problem exists, however, refer him to guidance for further discussion and evaluation.

5. This could be a very scary event for any classroom teacher! Keep youngsters away from the girl who has fainted. Immediately send a student with a pass to secure administrative and medical assistance. Gather the girl's possessions together and hold for the supervisor. Make every attempt to keep students in their seats. If not already done, open a nearby window to allow air to circulate.

6. The solution to this particular problem depends at what point during the class period it occurs. If the fire drill occurs shortly after the start of the period, but before you have begun the test, administer the short quiz upon the class' return to the room. There should be adequate time for completing the test. If the drill occurs during the quiz, and you feel quiz answers might be compromised, cancel the quiz, prepare a new one, and administer it during the next class meeting. On the other hand, a drill at the end of the period would most likely not interfere with your having given a quiz. A short quiz usually takes ten to twenty minutes to administer and probably would not cause a major dilemma under extraordinary circumstances.

7. This represents an 85% failure rate. This test result could indicate a lack of student mastery for a variety of reasons. The teacher would be well served to reexamine his/her teaching techniques, test design and in querying students in their study habits. In addition, spot check student notes to determine whether in-class note-taking is suspect. Perhaps chalkboard organization is faulty or unclear. Take a class survey to determine where possible problems might lie.

8. Explain to the student that he missed the deadline announced earlier during the term. Unless he has a medical excuse, in all fair conscience you cannot accept his paper. It is unfair to other students who have met the same required obligations. Explain further that he has a responsibility to meet all deadlines.

9. In this scenario you want to allay the parent's anger before defending yourself. Phone the parent. Tell her that you are sorry she is upset. Assure her that you are not biased against her daughter. Explain that the grade was determined, and agreed upon, by both her daughter and you in mutual consultation at an end-term class interview. Offer to reevaluate the student's term performance once again. Tell her you will call back shortly to explain findings. Document the complaint and the dates of your return phone call or written communication. If you determine that the final grade is justified, inform your subject supervisor of the situation. Let him/her advise you how to proceed from here.

10. If you note excessive cutting in a particular class, make a list of class cutters. Contact homes to inform parents of the cutting situation. Reevaluate your lessons from the time that the cutting became most apparent. Do you find any weaknesses in the motivation or questioning technique? Have you offered youngsters a variety of different lesson types? Are lessons intellectually challenging for students and/or adequately modified as the case might be?

The teacher communicates the need for social justice.

CONCLUSION

The contents of this primer provide the means for a teacher to enter a classroom free from the fear of not knowing what to do. The book alleviates to a large extent teacher anxiety. Its contents offer a foundation for launching classroom activities with confidence. It further provides the teacher with the capability of achieving both function and stability in the classroom.

The teacher must be a pragmatist! One should not be afraid of experimenting with new methods and techniques. Be flexible in adopting that which works while discarding or revising that which hinders the learning experience for youngsters. Allow experience to become your guide.

Students demand structure and discipline in the classroom. Be flexible in your approach to bothersome classroom situations as they arise. In addition, if a teacher mistake is made, when transmitting information or in one's perception of a situation, admit the error. When asked a question, for which you do not know an answer, admit that you don't know but will investigate and report back to the class.

Attend to all administrative matters required of your position with precision and efficiency. Administrative matters such as updating student statistics, and proctoring schoolwide and State mandated exams, are only a few of the necessary items for which a teacher is additionally responsible. Carry out these duties to the best of your ability, for they, too, reflect upon your professional stature.

The end of another school day!

A teacher prepares students for life.

A teacher shows kindness to youngsters.

Teacher Forms

FORM A: AN OPENING TERM CHECKLIST

Date_____

I have/have not secured the following necessary and immediate items from my supervisor for the opening of the new term:

	Yes	No
My term program		
Subject text/texts		
Room assignment keys		
Restroom key		
Opening day attendance lists		
A calendar of lessons		
Uniform homework sheets (if available)		
Attendance and record-keeping book		
Staff information booklet		
VCR inventory list		
Six absentee lessons with instructions		
Discipline referral forms (school form if available)		
School stationery and envelopes		
Content material (maps, test tubes, a chalkboard compass, etc.)		
Chalk, eraser and class pass		

FORM B

SEATING CHART

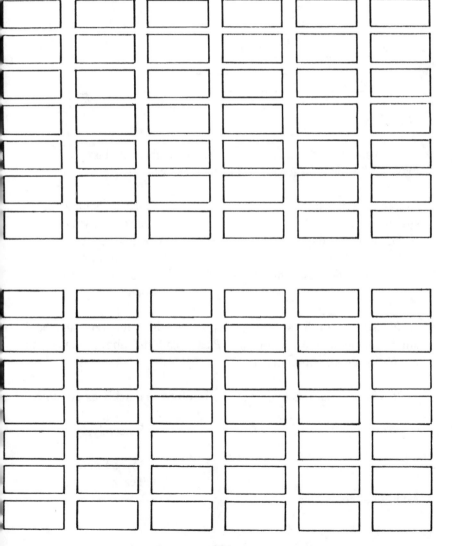

FORM C: A HOME CONTACT LETTER

John Brown High School
432 Franklin Street
Philadelphia, Pennsylvania 97100
Phone (326) 973-4200

Date_____

Mr./Ms._____

_____

_____

Dear Parent:

I am sorry to advise you that your son/daughter of class_____
may fail for the term for the following reasons:

---poor attendance	---missing homework
---cutting class	---lacks motivation
---absent on test days	---is unprepared
---is late to class	---poor test grades
---fails to hand-in assignments on time	---lacks self control
	---other_____

Please discuss the above checked items with your son/daughter. I
am available to meet with you. Please call the above number to
arrange a school appointment.

It is hoped that this matter can be resolved as quickly as possible.

Sincerely,

Joyce Smith
Teacher

Additional comments:

FORM D: INTER-SCHOOL MEMO

John Adams Junior High School
1714 Riverdale Avenue
Houston, Texas 89132

Date_____

To:_____

From:_____

Topic:_____

Dear_____:

_____
_____
_____
_____
_____
_____
_____
_____
_____
_____

Sincerely,

FORM E: INTER-SCHOOL DISCIPLINE REFERRAL

To:_____   Date_____

From:_____

Re: (student's name and class)

Dear_____:

Description of Complaint:

_____

_____

_____

_____

_____

_____

_____

_____

_____

_____

_____

_____

                                        Sincerely,

FORM F: EXCESSIVE ABSENCE FROM CLASS

John Smith High School
2001 Sycamore Road
Santa Fe, New Mexico 87293

_____19__

Dear Parent/Guardian:

Your son/daughter_____ has
been absent several times in (state the month). I have attempted to
contact you but cannot locate a working telephone number.

Would you be so kind as to call me at:

Telephone #(123) 456-7889, extension #15, during the hour 7:30-
8:30 AM.

Thank you.

Sincerely,

John Smith
Teacher

FORM G: EXCESSIVE ABSENCE FROM CLASS

Mary Jones Memorial High School
1155 Michigan Avenue
Flint, Michigan 56478

Date_____

Dear Parent/Guardian:

We regret to inform you that your son/daughter_____has
not been attending classes regularly. Continuous absence from
subject class_____can lead to failure and a delay of graduation.

Please discuss this matter with your son/daughter. For additional information please contact me, between the hours _____daily,
at (274) 789-1234.

Very truly yours,

Rachel Smith

FORM H: NOTIFICATION OF SUBJECT FAILURE

R.W. Rathbone Junior High School
1865 Rose Lane
Buffalo, New York 14538

Date_____

Dear Parent/Guardian:

Please be advised that your son/daughter_____
has failed subject_____ for this marking period. Would you
be so kind as to discuss this with your son/daughter.

Continued failure may result in having your child's graduation delayed.

If I may be of service to you in some way, please do not
hesitate to call me at (343) 678-1234 between the hours of 8:45-9:20
A.M. If I am unavailable when you call, please leave a message and I
will contact you shortly.

Sincerely,

Janet Bright

Teachers are visionary!

INDEX

Teacher Notes

Teacher Notes

Order Form

Please forward the following order for *__Teaching And The Art Of Successful Classroom Management, ISBN 0-9640602-2-1:__*

Number of books:_____($16.95 each) Canada ($21.95)

Organization name:_____

Name: (please print)_____

Address: _____

City:_____State:_____Zip:_____

Sales tax:
Please add 8.25% for books shipped in New York State.

Shipping:
Book rate: $_1.75____for the first book and__$1.25___ for each additional book. Please permit 3-4 weeks for postal delivery.
Air Mail: $__6.00_____per book.

Payment:
___ Check
___ Money Order

Please forward book orders to:

      Aysa Publishing, Inc.
      P.O. Box 131556
      Staten Island, New York 10313
      U.S.A.

For inquiries or additional information: **Phone & Fax (718) 370-3201**
I understand that I may return this book for a full refund, anytime, if I am not totally satisfied as long as the book is in good condition and still in print.